Ultimate Corvette Trivia Challenge

By Wallace A. Wyss
Introduction by Dick Guldstrand
Expert proofreaders:
    Dan Gale
    Wayne Ellwood
    Duke Williams

Iconografix

Iconografix, Inc.
PO Box 446
Hudson, Wisconsin 54016 USA

Iconografix books are offered at a discount when sold in quantity for promotional use. Businesses
or organizations seeking details should write to the Marketing Department, Iconografix, at the
above address.

Library of Congress Card Number: 00-135941

ISBN 1-58388-035-6

01 02 03 04 05 06 07 5 4 3 2 1

Printed in the United States of America

Cover and book design by Shawn Glidden

Copyediting by Dylan Frautschi

Book Proposals

Iconografix is a publishing company specializing
in books for transportation enthusiasts. We pub-
lish in a number of different areas, including
Automobiles, Auto Racing, Buses, Construction
Equipment, Emergency Equipment, Farming
Equipment, Railroads & Trucks. The Iconografix
imprint is constantly growing and expanding into
new subject areas.

Authors, editors, and knowledgeable enthusiasts
in the field of transportation history are invited to
contact the Editorial Department at Iconografix,
Inc., PO Box 446, Hudson, WI 54016.

Table of Contents:

Introduction

My life is Corvette questions, like "Which is better—the L88 or L89?" or "Should I get a ZR1 or a Callaway?"

And so on, from every state in the Union, and even a few foreign countries.

So when Wally Wyss asked me to review his Corvette quiz, I thought—what the hey, it's what I do every day at my shop, the shop I've run since I hung up my driving helmet 20-odd years ago.

But I don't normally think of Corvettes as option numbers. I think of the great memories I've had in Corvettes—doing 170 mph down the Mulsanne straight at LeMans, driving with Zora on the Proving Grounds, winning a race at Riverside in '66 in a car with no brakes. Driving a Corvette Grand Sport at Sebring.

And then I've got the more recent memories of the customers I've built cars for. The day they pick up their car, take it around the block, and come back with that grin on their face that means they've gotten a little closer to their performance fantasy.

And then there's the friends I've made among the people who've created the great Corvettes, engineers like Zora, Dave McLellan, Dave Hill, Jim Ingle. I've celebrated with them when they had a winner, and commiserated with them during the occasional dark days at GM when "performance" was a dirty word and we had to hide the Corvette race cars or the parts that made them faster.

And of course I count the designers as friends—Larry Shinoda, Jerry Palmer, John Cafaro, Chuck Jordan. Designers don't know what to do with me, because I'm an engineer but we get along. In fact, one time I commissioned my own Corvette design—the GS90—one done my way.

Overall, when I look back on my business career, I can explain why I've stuck with the Corvette through thick and thin (and some years, you could hardly call them a performance car). It's because I believed that they could be fun again. I was right. The current product has a lot of potential to make it as a world class sports car. I've got a few in my shop, doing a tweak here, a tweak there.

Now, this quiz. Well, I thought I could breeze through the Q & A, but the problem is that every few questions I hit another one that evokes one of those memories gleaned in 40 years of association with Corvettes. That's a lot of plastic down the road.

I hope it never stops.

Dick Guldstrand
Guldstrand Enterprises
Burbank, CA

A Word from the Proofreaders

It's been said the word "Corvette" refers to a Canadian naval patrol boat, somewhat smaller than a destroyer. The naval version of the Corvette is actually a vessel type rather than a specific ship series. I discuss this to show you us Canadians had something to do with the Corvette—even if originally it was only in the name.

But this book is about the Chevrolet Corvette—a subject near to my heart.

I can't really tell you when I first decided that this was the brand of automobile that was going to fulfill my needs for driving excitement. It was really quite late in life; not in my childhood, not in my teens, but well into my twenties. Like every other young man, I spent a lot of my high school class time dreaming about cars but back then it wasn't specific. It wasn't until the mid-'70s when I "locked in" on the Corvette as a world class sports car.

Those years marked some of the high points in Corvette racing. Race cars were still based on the actual vehicle chassis and roll cages were just roll bars. The Corvette was world class and it ran with the best. In North America, it dominated. Subsequent years were somewhat more difficult for Corvettes as tube frame race cars became the order of the day. The costs of racing escalated and the privateers who had raced Corvettes out of their own wallet dropped from the scene.

But it was too late for me—regardless of what happened in Corvette racing, the hook had been set. Although I was following a career as a Canadian Coast Guard officer, I embarked on a second career in the Corvette scene—at one time President of the Canadian Council of Corvette Clubs (Eastern Region). Someone liked the club magazine I did and suggested I start a magazine with him. We began SHARK Quarterly, and the year 2000 saw its fifth year of publication.

Once I became a magazine editor I began receiving mail about each article—pointing out finer details of the cars I'd discussed. It was then I found how particular Corvette fans are about the details in the Corvette's 50-year history.

Often I can tell the questions that come across my desk—such as "Where are the Motorama cars?" "What was the first year for a power top?", etc. are being asked not just for curiosity but because someone is about to make a buying decision, and my answer may help them decide before they take the plunge.

But this book is no buyer's guide. It's a fun exercise created by author Wally Wyss to test you and to tease you, both with trivia and fundamental facts. The book manages to get into the "Zeitgeist" of the times—such as what famous people owned Corvettes? Or who were some of the personalities that designed them? Or engineered them? Or raced them?

It's wide-open full-throttle fun. A portable challenge you can take along with you in your car, on a bus trip or plane. Open it at any page and challenge yourself. "Oh, I know the answer to that" you tell yourself. But, let me tell you, when I first saw the project, I too said: "Hey, duck soup, no problem." Wrong. By the time I got to question 300 I realized you had to have an arm's length of Corvette books memorized to know all the answers.

They're still making new Corvettes as you read this, and until they make the last one, knowledge of the subject can never be "complete." What you are holding in your hands right now is a great example of some of the finest trivia you are ever going to find. Please enjoy it.

Wayne Ellwood
Editor, SHARK quarterly
129 Dunbarton Court
Ottana, ON K1K4L6 Canada

Cars have always been in my blood—I've sold them, raced them, drag-raced them, rallied them, fixed them and even wrecked a few.

But one of the memories that stands out the strongest was when I was a kid, back in 1953, when my Dad took me to the Chevrolet dealership in a neighboring town. There I found my true love—a beautiful pristine new Corvette. It was love at first sight.

As the years went on, the Corvette hobby became more and more a part of my everyday life; not just a weekend joy. Then came this crazy idea—the National Corvette Museum. Taking on a project of this magnitude meant a full-time commitment. Again it was love at first sight. But with the Museum's grand opening in the fall of 1994, it was time for me to return to a more normal way of existence.

Through all of the changes life brings, I never lost my original love of the car. The Corvette is rich in history, mystique and charm—not to mention power and style. But most of all it brings joy to the owner. An ego trip that you can only experience—and never fully describe to the unknowing. It's a car for fun, fun, fun.

And so, too, as you read through this book, I urge you to have fun, fun, fun. Don't look for the hairline scratches, the wax build-up in the taillight lenses or the smudges on the windshield. Don't worry if the body panels aren't lined up exactly perfect. They never were in the first place! Instead, revel in the richness of the design, the brightness of its past and the diversity of its lineage. Enjoy learning about the men and women behind America's Only Sports Car. Test your suaveness. Surprise yourself. But most of all, take pleasure in the ride. That's what the Corvette is all about.

Dan Gale

Owning and driving a Corvette—any model year Corvette—is not like owning any other car. It's been variously described as a "lifestyle," a hobby, even an obsession. How many drivers know the name of their model's chief engineer and lead designers? Not only that, but Corvette owners often know the succession of chief engineers and designers throughout the Corvette's nearly 50-year history. Indeed, key Corvette personnel achieve true celebrity status, among the faithful. Beyond this there is a nearly limitless level of detail we can delve into, and often do. Options, particularly those rare engine and chassis options that were meant for serious racers are of particular interest, but this is just the beginning for the serious Corvette enthusiast.

My obsession for detail is motivated by the desire for a "correct" restoration and, in particular, I am interested in the history of the Corvette's technology—the "whys" and "wherefores" of its development—but technology itself does not define a Corvette. For much of its life, the Corvette was defined by strong-willed, single-minded men who had a strong vision of what the Corvette should look like and how it should perform. There's no way that the 1963 Sting Ray coupe could have been designed by a committee or sculpted by consumer clinics. It was the inspiration of one man—Bill Mitchell. Yes, the young Larry Shinoda did most of the renderings, but under Mitchell's guiding hand. Make no mistake—it was Mitchell's design.

Zora Arkus-Duntov's mission in life was to make the Corvette go—to make sure it had world class performance, and what he created is the stuff of legend—the prototypes, hemi-head engines and lightweight Corvettes. He was the "gatekeeper" of GM's infamous "back door" into racing. The political intrigues of dedicated and talented men to overcome the indifference and sometimes outright hostility of a faceless corporation would make a good novel.

The 1970s marked the end of the early glory days as the engineering emphasis refocused on safety and emissions. Though performance declined, sales went on to set new records. Following Zora's retirement, Dave McLellan had to spend his early years as Chief Engineer just updating the aging design to keep the Corvette in compliance with the myriad of new safety and emissions requirements. Once the pace of technology improvement overcame the volume of new Federal mandates and GM recovered from their financial crisis of the 1970s, Dave was free to design an all-new Corvette.

The "C4" brought the Corvette back to the roots established by Duntov. Performance was paramount, but comfort was a bit compromised, and quality was still not up to the level that customers desired. With time, the design was refined and spawned the highest technology and best performing Corvette ever—the ZR-1.

In the early 1990s a new Corvette program began, but again, financial difficulties at GM delayed the program for several years. Perhaps the delay was a blessing in disguise. It ultimately allowed additional design refinement and the incorporation of new technology. By this time the role of chief engineer had changed. Rather than the brilliant intuitive engineering genius of Duntov, a 1990s chief engineer had to manage and coordinate the vast personnel and technical resources that were available, and Dave Hill has done an enviable job. Computer-aided design tools allowed the investigation, optimization, and performance analysis of several design architectures without the time and expense of building hardware. Once the major high level design tasks were completed, numerous prototypes were built, and it was good, very good! By incorporating manufacturing personnel early in the design process, a highly manufacturable design was produced that resulted in a sports car with an unprecedented combination of performance, comfort, economy of operation, and value; and the "C5" ultimately eclipsed the performance of the legendary ZR-1 without the cost of its expensive hardware. As the Corvette approaches its 50th Anniversary, it maintains the distinction of having the most powerful and enduring legacy of any American marque and will likely enjoy another 50 years of success.

Meanwhile, the quest for knowledge continues. Years from now when our sons and grandsons (and maybe some daughters and granddaughters) begin restoring C4s and C5s, the inherent complexity relative to the early models may be partially offset by previous generations of restorers and enthusiasts who unlocked the secrets of date-coded parts and finishing materials. Unfortunately, the individual build records for the Corvettes produced at St. Louis appear to be lost, so with the exception of original purchase records kept by owners and "tank stickers" that are recovered from 1967 and up models, the original option configuration of many Corvettes may never be known. The National Corvette Museum now archives the individual build (or "broadcast") sheets for all Corvettes built at Bowling Green since production began there in 1981, so future restorers will know exactly what equipment and options were installed on their specific VIN. However, it probably remains for some future restorer to determine the "correct" type and shade of paint to restore the red finish on those 2001 Z06 brake calipers...

Duke Williams
Redondo Beach, CA
December 2000

Acknowledgments

Special thanks to the members of the on-line forums who endured being barraged with questions including www.CorvetteForum.com and www.NCRS.org. Thanks also to those who read portions of the manuscript: Duke Williams, owner of a pristine '63 and an encyclopedic-like mind; Allen Hickey, Jr. of Louisiana, Jeff Smith, owner of an L88/M4, Dick Guldstrand and Jim Gessner of Guldstrand Engineering Inc. Culver City, CA, Ron Miklos of Pittsburgh, PA, and Mike Scott of Corvette Corrections in Anaheim, CA. Also, thanks to "Corvette Mike" Vietro of Anaheim, CA.

A Word from the Editor

I owned a Corvette once, some thirty years ago. It was a '69 coupe. I never thought of it as Option A31, with Option A82 and so forth. Naw—to me it was the canary yellow (oops, Daytona Yellow) coupe beckoning from my driveway.

Flash forward 30 years. I'm driving around wondering—if you've got every Corvette book imaginable on your bookshelf, what one would you still need?

This book is the result. It tests what you know, or what you think you know.

Like Dick Guldstrand, I have a hard time sticking to the questions because memories keep intruding, like the first time I saw a '57 at the Franklin Cider Mill in Franklin, Michigan. Or the time I rode in one of the Owens-Corning Corvettes to the grid at Brainerd, Minnesota, or the time Bill Mitchell took me for a ride in the Shark and later, the Mako Shark II.

I agree it's important to know what options were available when because you want to know how original a car is before you buy it. The books listed in the bibliography (particularly the Corvette Black Book) will help you there. This book is more for the fun of it...

The Editor and proofreaders have made every effort to ensure that the "correct" answers are indeed correct. But with conflicting information gathered from "historians" of varying skill and scholarship, we concede that there is some room for error.

Wallace A. Wyss.
Malibu, CA

Why the Questions are not in Chronological Order

Some of the answers involve guessing the right year an option was offered. If we kept to strict chronological order, we would make it too easy on you. Suffer.

A Note Regarding Usage

Chevrolet has gone both ways at various times on whether to use a hyphen between the alphabetical letters of a Regular Production Option (RPO) and the number of the option, i.e. L-88. We chose to delete the hyphen. We also chose to insert a space between the alphabetical and numerical portions for easier readability.

How to Take The Corvette Trivia Challenge

1. Don't bet anyone you can complete it in an hour.

2. If you're ready, mark your answer. If you aren't ready, read the Inside Scoop section (starting on page 70) first to expand your knowledge.

3. Follow the scoring card on page 10 for scoring the Q & A section.

4. Read the Inside Scoop section for the ones you got wrong to expand your knowledge.

5. Read the Inside Scoop section straight through. As the name implies, you will get the "inside scoop" on all 300 Q&As. Yes, this section gives you expanded answers to all the questions and explains why the right answer is right. Even if you scored close to 100% in the Q&A section, you are guaranteed to find information you didn't know. You will learn a lot about eras that you aren't familiar with and find interesting facts to challenge your friends.

.

SCORE CARD directions: Record the number of correct answers you gave for each era below, however, don't include Bonus Questions in each era. Write the number of total Bonus Questions you got correct on the line marked "*Bonus Questions" below (these are "freebies" and do not effect your score negatively). Add up your correct responses and divide the total by 300, then multiply by 100. Compare your score with your friends to assess your "bragging rights!" Good luck, and remember, these questions are challenging…

The Boulevardier Years .... ____ out of 15 questions

Zora Targets the 300SL .... ____ out of 41 questions

The Duck-Tail Era .... ____ out of 15 questions

The Sting Ray Era .... ____ out of 73 questions

The Mako Shark Era .... ____ out of 96 questions

The C4 Era .... ____ out of 54 questions

The C5 Era .... ____ out of 6 questions

*Bonus Questions .... ____ out of 14 questions

Total Correct .... ____/300x100 = ____ %

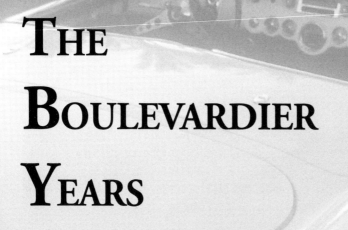

THE

BOULEVARDIER

YEARS

Bonus Question: The big "V" (shown in the above photo) meant what in 1955?

    a.) "V" for victory over Ford's T-birds   c.) No meaning other than décor
    b.) "V" for V-8 option

1. The name "Corvette" was in use by the military before there were cars existent. What type of vehicle did it refer to?

    a.) airplane   c.) self-propelled howitzer
    b.) ship   d.) tank

2. As GM was thinking of making their sports car, the following 2-seater sports cars were already being sold in America except for which one?

    a.) Nash-Healey   c.) Kaiser-Darrin
    b.) Cunningham   d.) Scarab

3. What were mandatory "options" on the '53 Corvette? (Hint: more than one answer.)

    a.) Signal Seeking radio   c.) hardtop
    b.) heater   d.) full wheel covers

Bonus Question: b.) "V" for V-8 options, 1: b, 2: d, 3: a & b,

4. Corvettes were in short supply in 1953 so GM decided to sell them only to the rich and famous to extract maximum publicity value. What was one American family that got three of them?

a.) the Rockefellers   c.) the Trumps
b.) the Mellons   d.) the DuPonts

5. Which Corvette engine was heavier in 1955?

a.) Blue Flame six   b.) the 265 cu. in. V-8

6. How many separate body pieces were there for the '53 Corvette?

a.) 104   c.) 46
b.) 6   d.) 53

7. If you are doing a body-off restoration on your '53-'55 Corvette, you might need more than four buddies to lift the body off the frame. It weighed:

a.) 320 lbs   c.) 530 lbs
b.) 411 lbs   d.) 610 lbs

8. The Corvette originally came with only one color interior—red. By 1954 there was a second color added. What was it?

a.) black   c.) white
b.) beige

9. Which manufacturer made the frame for the '53 Corvette?

a.) Fisher Body   c.) A.O. Smith
b.) GM Stamping   d.) Owens-Corning

10. The supplier of fiberglass body parts for Chevrolet in 1953 was:

a.) Fisher Body   c.) Rockwell
b.) Molded Fiber Glass Co.   d.) Owens Corning

11. The radio antenna on the '53 Corvettes was found in what unusual place?

a.) rear deck lid   c.) windshield frame
b.) front right fender   d.) gas cap lid

4: d, 5: a, 6: c, 7: b, 8: b, 9: c, 10: b, 11: a.

12. What features of the '53 Corvette were found on the first production Dodge Viper more than 30 years later? Clue: there's more than one right answer.

    a.) plastic body   c.) 6-volt battery
    b.) plastic side curtains

13. Who is the true father of the Corvette?

    a.) Zora Arkus-Duntov   c.) Harley Earl
    b.) Maurice Olley   d.) Bob McLean

14. Which model year in the early years saw leftover unsold Corvettes?

    a.) 1953   c.) 1955
    b.) 1954   d.) 1956

15. The Corvette enjoyed two years of being America's only domestic sports car, but then the Blue Oval folks over in Dearborn spoiled that by introducing the 2-seat Thunderbird in 1955. The first year both 2-seaters were on the market, which one outsold the other?

    a.) Corvette   b.) Thunderbird

Bonus Question: The Corvette's first plant was a pilot production operation where the cars were made by hand. Only 300 were built that first year. The first Corvettes, as shown in the above photo, were made in:

    a.) St. Louis, MO   c.) Flint, MI
    b.) Warren, MI

12: a & b, 13: c, 14: b, 15: b, Bonus Question: c.) Flint, MI

ZORA TARGETS THE 300SL

Zora Targets the 300SL

Bonus Question: The factory race car—seen here at the Monterey Historic races—was based on a '56 Corvette. It was called the:

a.) SS   c.) Corvette LeMans
b.) SR2   d.) Duntov Special

16. Zora Arkus-Duntov, the legendary Corvette engineer, came on board at GM in:

a.) May, 1952   c.) April, 1954
b.) May, 1953   d.) May, 1955

17. In 1955, when Chevy began to offer the V-8 in the Corvette, the six-cylinder got what?

a.) a 12-volt system   c.) fuel injection
b.) a supercharger   d.) none of the above

18. The over one-million-dollar special that was built by Chevrolet for the 1957 Sebring race was called the:

a.) SR1   c.) SS
b.) SR2   d.) Stingray Special

19. When you ordered "dual quads" on a Corvette, you received:

a.) twin 4-barrel carburetors   c.) a 2-barrel carburetor
b.) eight tail lamps   d.) twin disc brake calipers in the rear

Bonus Question: b.) SR2, 16: b, 17: d, 18: c, 19: a,

20. What famous cowboy hat-wearing mechanic did the prep work on the three '56 factory-owned Corvette beach racers run on the packed sands of Daytona Beach, Florida?

a.) Junior Johnson
b.) Salt Walther
c.) Fireball Roberts
d.) Smokey Yunick
e.) Max Balchowsky

21. What year saw the biggest year-to-year sales increase in Corvettes during the twentieth century?

a.) 1954
b.) 1956
c.) 1963
d.) 1984

22. The '57 "Airbox" cars relocated the tachometer to: .

a.) the passenger side
b.) atop steering column
c.) atop dash in a pod a la Shelby GT-350 in 1965
d.) the hood in special shroud a la Pontiac GTO

23. The Corvette heavy-duty racing package of 1957 was coded:

a.) RPO 684
b.) RPO Z01
c.) RPO X84
d.) RPO SR2

24. In 1957, the optional wide wheels, RPO 276, were what width?

a.) 5 inches
b.) 5.5 inches
c.) 6.6 inches
d.) 6.5 inches

25. "Metallics" referred to:

a.) Corvette cold air box in racing package
b.) Ram Jet fuel injection manifold
c.) ceramic moldings for headlight
d.) HD brake linings

26. In the mid-1950s, what annual production target did GM figure they needed to reach in order for the Corvette to make a profit?

a.) 10,000
b.) 12,000
c.) 50,000

Zora Targets the 300SL

27. Zora Arkus-Duntov and his brother first became known to American hot rodders when they developed a conversion head for the flathead Ford called:

    a.) Ardun   c.) Rajo
    b.) Al-Fin   d.) Fronty

28. Of the years below, which year was the big sales winner?

    a.) 1956   b.) 1957

29. In 1957, if you ordered fuel injection, you wanted to let everyone know you had Chevy's new secret weapon. Where was an emblem proclaiming fuel injection not put on the cars so equipped?

    a.) on each side cove   c.) on the nose of the car
    b.) on the trunk lid

30. What was the paint color choice ordered on the fewest '57 Corvette's?

    a.) Venetian Red   e.) Aztec Copper
    b.) Onyx black   f.) Cascade Green
    c.) Polo White   g.) Arctic Blue
    d.) Inca Silver

31. Old Corvette dream cars never die, they just reappear in new guises. Jim Jeffords, sponsored by Nickey Chevrolet of Chicago, raced the ex-Jerry Earl's SR2 in SCCA B-Production racing, winning a national title in the late 1950s. He named the car after a popular song. What was the title of that forgettable little ditty?

    a.) "The Little Engine that Could"   c.) "Purple People Eater"
    b.) "Dream Lover"   d.) "Jumpin' Jack Flash"

32. Bill Mitchell, VP in charge of styling at GM, and Harley Earl, his former boss, both shared passions for the things below except Mitchell alone liked:

    a.) Panama hats   d.) superchargers
    b.) side exhausts   e.) motorcycles
    c.) aircraft-inspired gauges   f.) tailfins

33. The side coves in the '56 were first previewed on what GM-built show cars? Clue: there's more than one right answer.

    a.) Biscayne   c.) Firebird I
    b.) LaSalle II   d.) Firebird III

34. GM unveiled several 2-seater show cars at their Motorama road shows in the mid-1950s. Which of the cars listed below was not a Motorama 2-seater show car?

a.) LeSabre
b.) Cadillac LeMans
c.) Buick Wildcat II
d.) Corvette Impala
e.) Chevrolet Corvette
f.) Oldsmobile F88

35. The following options were available with the "airbox" '57 Corvettes, except for one (which we put in this list to cause consternation). Can you spot our ringer?

a.) RPO 275 5.5-inch wide wheels
b.) RPO 678 Positraction, 4.11 ratio
c.) RPO 685 4-speed transmission
d.) RPO 684 HD racing suspension and brakes
e.) RPO 378 bullet-shaped covers for the front headlamps

36. The '56 and '57 had what characteristic about their upholstery?

a.) alternating stripes of color
b.) simulated animal skin of some animal that never existed
c.) a pattern that looked like a waffle iron
d.) diamond-tufted

37. What kind of paint was on the '58 Corvette?

a.) nitrocellulose lacquer
b.) enamel
c.) acrylic lacquer
d.) water-based paint

38. In 1956, the good news was that you got the removable top (RPO 419) at no charge if you didn't want the soft-top. If you decided you also wanted the soft-top tucked away under the hardtop, how much extra did you have to pay?

a.) $10.00
b.) $202.30
c.) $215.20
d.) $528.13

39. The Wonder Bar radio of 1956 was earthshaking, state-of-the-art, cutting-edge technology in that it used:

a.) transistors
b.) FM
c.) Citizen's Band
d.) short-wave

40. What 1950s Corvette factory show car made only a brief appearance in auto shows, slipped into private hands, and then disappeared from public view for more than 40 years?

a.) Corvette Biscayne
b.) Corvette Super Sport
c.) Corvette SS race car
d.) Corvette XP-882

41. Which VIP bought a Corvette in 1956 with the "trunk irons" zooming up the trunk lid like the '58 Corvette?

a.) Harley Earl
b.) Bill Mitchell
c.) Zora Duntov
d.) Prince Bertil of Sweden

42. RPO 579E makes a '57 Corvette very valuable if you can document that it's original. RPO 579E refers to:

a.) dual racing plexi windscreens
b.) driver's headrest fairing
c.) 4-speed transmission
d.) fresh air intake and mechanical tachometer on steering column

43. Inventor of the Corvette's fuel injection system was:

a.) "Boss" Kettering
b.) Zora Arkus-Duntov
c.) John Dolza
d.) Stu Hilborn

44. In 1957, Ram Jet-style fuel injection was offered on other GM cars than Chevrolets. Which other GM marque below offered F.I. as an option in 1957?

a.) Buick
c.) Cadillac
b.) Oldsmobile
d.) Pontiac

45. Of the colors listed below, which was not an exterior color choice in 1957?

a.) Aztec Copper
b.) Cascade Green
c.) Venetian Red
d.) Inca Silver
e.) Topaz Blue

46. In 1960, when you ordered the Duntov-cammed 270-bhp twin carburetor engine, the tachometer came redlined at what rpm?

a.) 5,500 rpm
b.) 6,500 rpm
c.) 6,000 rpm

47. In 1956 RPO 440 referred to Corvettes with:

a.) 4-speeds
b.) the airbox
c.) two-tone paint
d.) hardtops

41: d, 42: d, 43: c, 44: d, 45: e, 46: b, 47: c.

48. Corvettes were occasionally re-bodied in Italy from the 1950s to the 1990s. Some of the carrozzerias (CA-ROTZ-ZOH-RHEE-UH) or coachbuilders listed below had bodied at least one Corvette. Which ones? Clue: there's more than one right answer.

a.) Scaglietti
b.) Vignale
c.) Bertone
d.) Pininfarina
e.) Zagato
f.) Frua

49. According to noted Corvette historian Noland Adams, what option was offered in 1957 to Corvette racers from the factory though not listed on any option lists?

a.) aluminum block
b.) Halibrand wheels
c.) 24-gallon gas tank
d.) lightweight body

50. The '59 Corvette basically used the 1958 body style, though the trunk irons zooming up the trunk lid had disappeared. What new thing was added to the interior?

a.) chronometer
b.) chrome shift knob
c.) storage bin under grab bar

51. The T-shaped reverse lock-out handle just below the knob on the gearshift first appeared in:

a.) 1956
b.) 1957
c.) 1958
d.) 1959

52. Fuel injection of the original Rochester Ram Jet type had its highs and lows in popularity. Below you'll find what are reported to be accurate sales figures with the exception of a ringer (false entry). Can you spot the false sales figure?

a.) 1957: 1,040
b.) 1958: 1,511
c.) 1959: 1,092
d.) 1960: 659
e.) 1961: 1,580
f.) 1962: 1,918
g.) 1963: 2,610
h.) 1964: 1,325
i.) 1965: 771
j.) 1966: 421

53. RPO 686, available in 1959, referred to:

a.) aluminum head option
b.) power convertible top option
c.) metallic brake linings
d.) the Wonder Bar radio

48: a, b, c & d, 49: c, 50: c, 51: d, 52: j, 53: c,

Zora Targets the 300SL

54. Which American millionaire took a team of Corvettes to race at the 24 Hours of LeMans in France in June 1960?

a.) Lance Reventlow   c.) Briggs Swift Cunningham
b.) Tommy Manville   d.) "Gentleman Jim" Kimberley

55. The '59 Corvette's coves were available in which of the contrasting colors listed? (Clue: more than one answer)

a.) Silver   c.) Black
b.) White   d.) Red

56. In 1959 what soft-top color was offered that never reappeared in the "solid axle days?"

a.) Blue-gray   c.) Turquoise
b.) White   d.) Beige

Bonus Question: The dual hood blisters, seen in the above photo, were a styling inspiration from what foreign sports car? The car in general inspired the '56 Corvette and also led GM to offer fuel injection.

a.) Pegaso Z-108   c.) BMW 507
b.) Jaguar XK-120   d.) Mercedes 300SL gullwing

THE
DUCK - TAIL
ERA

The Duck-Tail Era

Bonus Question: The above car was commissioned by William L. Mitchell as his private car, but his boss, Harley Earl, recognized its merits and had it commissioned as an official GM show car. The grille was redesigned and the colors changed in the update. The name of this prototype, which inspired the '61-'62 duck-tail, was the:

a) XP-500
b) XP-700

c) XP-1000
d) EX-122

57. What did the contrasting coves cost in 1961?

a.) $54.20
b.) $16.15

c.) $45.13
d.) $240.00

58. What was the last year for wide whitewalls on the Corvette?

a.) 1957
b.) 1960

c.) 1961
d.) 1962

59. For many years, chrome grilles were the standard. Then suddenly Chevrolet discovered anodizing chrome and blacking out chrome. What year saw that first applied on the Corvette?

a.) 1960
b.) 1961

c.) 1962
d.) 1963

60. In 1962, the Corvette engine went from 283 cu. in. to:

a.) 358 cu. in.
b.) 327 cu. in.

c.) 302 cu. in.
d.) 409 cu. in.

Bonus Question: b.) XP-700, 57: b, 58: c, 59: c, 60: b,

61. What model year did the Corvette pass the "break-even point" to where it started making a profit?

a.) 1958
b.) 1960
c.) 1961
d.) 1963

62. What was the last year for the competition style 3-spoke aluminum steering wheel with drilled holes that had been around since 1956?

a.) 1961
b.) 1962
c.) 1963
d.) 1964
e.) all of the above

63. In 1962, when you ordered the higher performance 340 or 360-hp engines, what result did that show in the interior?

a.) heavy-duty seat belts
b.) 160 mph speedometer
c.) tachometer redline of 6,500 rpm
d.) metal mats on floor instead of vinyl

64. What was the purpose of the small aluminum keg placed horizontally under the hood of some '61 Corvettes? (The one that looks like a mini-beer keg.)

a.) windshield washer fluid
b.) water injection to cool heads
c.) hot water for heating system
d.) remote expansion tank

65. In 1962, the side view of the stock Corvette was enhanced by what factory accessory:

a.) sidemount exhausts
b.) Dayton wire wheels
c.) Vinyl-covered hardtop
d.) Rocker panel molding of ribbed aluminum

66. When Chevrolet went to the duck-tail styling on the rear of the '61, what percentage did they gain in luggage space?

a.) 10%
b.) 15%
c.) 20%

67. In 1962, what former option became standard, making the Corvette more civilized?

a.) foam cushion seats
b.) fitted luggage
c.) flock-lined trunk
d.) heater/defroster

61: c, 62: b, 63: c, 64: d, 65: d, 66: c, 67: d.

68. Which year Corvette was the last year to have contrasting coves?

    a.) 1961   c.) 1958
    b.) 1962   d.) 1957

69. Cosmetic changes on '62 Corvettes included the following except:

    a.) rectangular emblem on fender for fuel-injected cars
    b.) multi-rib extrusion on edge of reverse scoop in coves.
    c.) deletion of chrome trim around cove
    d.) black chrome shift lever on manual

70. Which of the drivers named below were SCCA B-production competitors in Corvettes in 1962? Clue: there's more than one right answer.

    a.) Roger Penske   c.) Don Yenko
    b.) Lance Reventlow   d.) Frank Dominianni

71. Although duck-tails are pretty similar in 1961 and 1962, what interior color was dropped after 1961?

    a.) black   c.) fawn
    b.) red   d.) blue

Bonus Question: This duck-tail, which does not have a chrome surround outlining the "cove," and has a vertical chrome-ribbed piece of trim in the cove is an example of what model year?

    a) 1961   b) 1962

68: a, 69: d, 70: c & d, 71: d, Bonus Question: b.) 1962

THE STING RAY ERA

The Sting Ray Era

(Photo courtesy Duke Williams)

Bonus Question: The split rear window shown above on the Sting Ray coupe was only featured one year. Bill Mitchell wanted the feature but criticism of it caused GM to drop it the following year. What year was it offered?

a) 1963
b) 1964
c) 1965
d) 1966
e) 1967

72. Which of the following model years saw a jump in sales of almost 50% from the year before?

a.) 1955
b.) 1963
c.) 1966
d.) 1973

73. The car shown by GM today as the "Mako Shark I" was originally billed as the:

a.) Shark
b.) Q-Corvette
c.) Stingray Special

74. Semon "Bunkie" Knudsen, a GM executive who liked racing, planned to build how many Grand Sport coupes for the 1963 racing season?

a.) 100
b.) 125
c.) 1,500
d.) 5

Bonus Question: a.) 1963, 72: b, 73: a, 74: b,

75. The original Grand Sport race cars of 1963 were planned to have engines displacing:

a.) 327 cu. in.
b.) 350 cu. in.
c.) 377 cu. in.
d.) 402 cu. in.

76. Which two key personalities in Corvette history—one from the 1950s, and one from the 1960s—both spent a portion of WWII behind barbed wire?

a.) Zora Arkus-Duntov
b.) John Fitch
c.) Larry Shinoda
d.) Bill Mitchell

77. The first year an AM/FM radio was offered in the Corvette was:

a.) 1960
b.) 1963
c.) 1964
d.) 1968

78. Elvis Aaron Presley (one-time Tupelo, Mississippi, truck driver who later became the King of the crooners) was seen in the title sequence of one of his films driving the Stingray Special, in the red livery it temporarily wore (at a time when it was also fitted with a 427 with four Webers visible through a clear bubble air scoop). What was the movie?

a.) "Spinout"
b.) "Clambake"
c.) "Speedway"
d.) "Viva Las Vegas"

79. The concept car called the Shark early in its career and Mako Shark I later in its career was built upon the chassis of what other concept car, extinguishing that earlier car's career forever?

a.) XP-700
b.) XP-755
c.) XP-880
d.) XP-882

80. GM's legal eagles have nightmares about GM prototypes being in private hands. Yet they lost several through the decades. Which show cars or prototypes below represent cars "lost" from their vaults?

a.) XP-819 rear-engined Corvette
b.) CERV I single-seater
c.) CERV II 4WD
d.) all SRs
g.) all Grand Sports
h.) all of the above

81. The biggest help in reducing unsprung weight in the '63 Sting Ray production car was due to the use of which of the items listed below?

a.) aluminum block
b.) independent rear suspension
c.) aluminum bumpers
d.) aluminum frame

82. The Corvette was dominant in American SCCA racing in 1961 and 1962, but another car came along in 1962 to threaten it, taking firm hold in racing in 1964. That was the:

a.) Porsche Speedster
b.) Shelby Cobra
c.) Scarab
d.) Bocar

83. The split rear window of the '63 Corvette coupe was previewed nearly a decade in advance on which postwar GM show car?

a.) Olds Golden Rocket
b.) Buick Silver Arrow
c.) Buick Wildcat II
d.) Olds F-88

84. Which of the following features of the '63 Sting Ray production car were simulated?

a.) hood louvers
b.) knock-offs on the hubcaps
c.) fender vents
d.) B-pillar air extraction vents
e.) all of the above

85. Which was the more popular body style in the 1963 model year, the first for the "Sting Ray" production car?

a.) coupe
b.) convertible

86. How many of the original Grand Sport racing Corvettes were originally built as roadsters?

a.) two
b.) five
c.) three
d.) zero

87. Harley Earl, former VP in Charge of Styling (before the word "Styling" was changed to the classier word "Design") retired in 1958, but his friends at Design staff gifted him with a '63 Sting Ray convertible equipped with all the equipment below except for what?

a.) Kelsey Hayes aluminum wheels
b.) 2-bar knock-of
c.) roof periscope
d.) extra gauges on passenger side of dashboard including altimeter
e.) Shark show car-style chrome pipes coming out of front fenders

81: b, 82: b, 83: a, 84: e, 85: b, 86: d, 87: c,

88. The Muncie gearbox, named after a town in Indiana, replaced the Borg-Warner 4-speed in late 1963. What was the first gear ratio in the wide-ratio Muncie that year?

a.) 2.54 c.) 2.57
b.) 2.56 d.) 2.58

89. The racing debut of the '63 Z06 coupe was at Riverside, at the Los Angeles Times Invitational Grand Prix, on October 13, 1962. Which of the drivers listed below was not one of the lucky drivers piloting a new Z06 in this event?

a.) Dave MacDonald d.) Doug Hooper
b.) Bob Bondurant e.) Mickey Thompson
c.) Jerry Grant

90. What options normally found on luxury cars didn't become Corvette options until 1963 with the introduction of the production Sting Ray? Hint: there's more than one right answer here.

a.) leather c.) air conditioning
b.) fitted luggage d.) power windows

91. The hotly sought-after Kelsey Hayes knock-offs first shown in 1963 were still available in 1966, but how many brave souls actually ordered PRO P48 in 1966?

a.) 25 c.) 1,455
b.) 104 d.) 1,194

92. At its debut, the Corvette Shark show car originally had what for an engine?

a.) 327 with one carburetor c.) 427 ZL1
b.) 327 with Roots supercharger
and two sidedraft carburetors

93. The Corvette Grand Sport race cars, at one time or another, used what parts not made by GM? Clue: there's more than one right answer.

a.) Halibrand wheels c.) Girling disc brakes
b.) 377 cu. in. V-8 d.) Weber carburetion

The Sting Ray Era

94. When the first three Grand Sports were smuggled out to Chevy's racing friends, what key ingredient did not go with them?

a.) lightweight body (replica of '63 production body)
b.) special handmade frames
c.) Halibrand knock-off wheels
d.) 377 cu. in. V-8

95. There was a 4-seater prototype built of the 1963 Corvette because someone believed it would "expand the market." Who at GM was the champion of this 4-seater?

a.) Zora Arkus-Duntov, Corvette Chief Engineer
b.) Bill Mitchell, VP in charge of Styling
c.) Ed Cole, General Manager, Chevrolet

96. Zora Arkus-Duntov tested the independent rear suspension (I.R.S.) design for the '63 Corvette on which engineering prototype?

a.) CERV II
b.) CERV I
c.) Monza GT
d.) GSllb

97. In the case of a '63 Corvette, what rare option could you show your car with that looks wrong, but is technically correct?

a.) 2-bar knock-offs
b.) 3-bar knock-offs
c.) vinyl-covered hardtop

98. What was the problem with '63 Sting Rays ordered with cast aluminum Kelsey-Hayes knock-off wheels?

a.) the wheels cracked
b.) the wheels were porous and leaked air
c.) the bars on the retaining nut shattered when you hit them with a hammer

99. The first year of the Sting Ray production car saw several racetrack-theme colors on the color palette. Several are listed below except for one "ringer." Which of the below is not a 1963 color?

a.) Mulsanne Maroon
b.) Daytona Blue
c.) Riverside Red
d.) Sebring Silver

100. What feature premiering on the '63 made the Corvette more comparable with the sophisticated sports cars of Europe?

a.) fuel injection
b.) disc brakes
c.) independent rear suspension
d.) radial tires

101. Very early '63 Sting Rays had what atop the new bolt-on top of the F. I. plenum chamber?

a.) letters "F. I."
b.) letter "W"
c.) letters "CORVETTE"
d.) numbers "327"

102. In 1964 a new addition to the interior was a:

a.) black chrome shift knob
b.) bright chrome-plated shift knob
c.) teak wood steering wheel
d.) silver interior

103. On the 1964 model, what improvements were added to enhance ride quality? Note: there is more than one right answer.

a.) rubber cushioned body-mounts
b.) variable rate springs
c.) gas-filled shock absorbers
d.) air pumps for bladders in seats to inflate seat cushions

104. What previously simulated styling feature from the '63 Corvette was made functional in 1964?

a.) B-pillar vents
b.) hood vents
c.) fender vents

105. In 1964 what oddball thing happened during production?

a.) 24 cars came with hardtops welded in place
b.) some F. I. cars got F. I. air filters from regular Chevrolets
c.) some knock-off wheel cars got knock-offs in front but not in back
d.) 24 cars were shipped out in primer; without paint

106. Of the 22,000 Corvettes made in 1964, a mere 806 had:

a.) fuel injection
b.) knock-off aluminum wheels
c.) A/C
d.) 36.5-gallon fuel tank

107. Millions who attended the 1964 World's Fair saw a metallic candy apple red Corvette coupe at the GM display. Which entry below was not among the list of features of this one-off show car?

a.) six taillights
b.) non-functional but beautiful side pipes emerging from a hole in front fenders and descending to become side exhausts
c.) knock-off wheels
d.) big block
e.) fuel injection unit rising from hole in hood

101: b, 102: b, 103: a & b, 104: a, 105: d, 106: b, 107: d.

108. The side-mount exhaust was introduced in:

    a.) 1963   c.) 1965
    b.) 1964   d.) 1966

109. The 1965 Corvette had all of the following except:

    a.) domed hood to clear   c.) drum brake availability
        air cleaner on big block   d.) 3-speed manual transmission
    b.) 390-hp big block option

110. What did drag racers nickname the big block?

    a.) elephant motor   c.) rat motor
    b.) calliope   d.) hemi

111. Which of the following years marked the last year a Carter carburetor was offered in the Corvette?

    a.) 1963   c.) 1965
    b.) 1964   d.) 1966

112. Shocking as it is, not all of the Corvette bodies from 1964-1967 were made by Chevrolet. In fact, about half of them came from an outside supplier in Michigan, the same supplier who later built Shelby Mustangs from mid-1967 on. That supplier was:

    a.) Fisher body   c.) Hamtramck Stamping
    b.) A.O. Smith   d.) Creative Industries

113. If you insisted, you could still get drum brakes on the '65. How much did Chevy give you back in credit if you insisted on the drums?

    a.) $120.10   c.) $64.50
    b.) $75.10   d.) $1,021.00

114. And speaking of those drum brakes again, how many '65 Corvettes were ordered with drum brakes?

    a.) 1,016   c.) 24
    b.) 316   d.) 2,422

108: c, 109: b, 110: c, 111: c, 112: b, 113: c, 114: b,

115. What made the 1966 Corvette different in badging than the '65?

a.) the badges were black instead of chrome

b.) there were no name badges

c.) the '66 had the words "Corvette Sting Ray" on the hood instead of the body

116. What was an unusual feature of the 1966 and 1967 427s with Powerglide and A/C?

a.) a front spoiler

b.) an electric cooling fan

c.) an offset license plate bracket to get more air into the grille cavity

117. What was the official designation for the gearbox known as the "rock crusher?"

a.) M20

b.) M22

c.) M30

d.) M80

118. The big block 396 offered in 1965 boasted all of the features below except for which one?

a.) aluminum heads

b.) 4-bolt mains

c.) impact extruded aluminum pistons

d.) Holley Type 4150 carburetor

e.) RPO K66 Transistor Ignition

119. What year did Dick Guldstrand and Bob Bondurant race a Corvette L88 coupe at LeMans?

a.) 1967

b.) 1968

c.) 1969

120. In 1965, when the big block made its debut, what was the weight distribution in the big block Corvette?

a.) 50/50

b.) 51/49

c.) 54/46

d.) 60/40

121. In 1965, fresh air fiends had their way and the majority of Corvettes ordered were convertibles. Out of 23,562 Corvettes made that year, how many were coupes?

a.) 9,200

b.) 10,123

c.) 8,186

d.) 240

122. The L88 introduced in 1967 had a Holley 4-barrel carburetor rated at:

a.) 550 cfm   c.) 750 cfm
b.) 650 cfm   d.) 850 cfm

123. The "big block" for 1966 displaced how many cubic inches?

a.) 396 cu. in.   c.) 403 cu. in.
b.) 427 cu. in.   d.) 409 cu. in.

124. The '66 coupe looked fairly similar to the '65, but what gimmick on the '65 was eliminated by 1966?

a.) fender vents   c.) vents on the roof pillars
b.) hood hump on the big block   d.) wraparound rear window

125. The L88s left off what item, which would have been handy for street driving?

a.) the air filter   c.) the emergency brake
b.) the radiator   d.) the choke

126. For 1967, in a departure from their usual practice, in the L88, GM gave very specific recommendations in a paper label on the console to tell you what fuel was required. What was the octane rating they recommended for this thirsty beast?

a.) 90   c.) 103
b.) 85   d.) 105

127. How many L88-equipped Corvettes do factory records show were built in 1967?

a.) 188   c.) 100
b.) 20   d.) 1,023

128. In 1966, how many customers buying L72s went for the M22 rock crusher?

a.) 230   c.) 22
b.) 15   d.) 1,047

129. In 1967, the L71 435-hp option cost $437.00. If you wanted aluminum heads as well, how much more did that add to the cost?

a.) $20   c.) $45
b.) $368   d.) $920

122: d, 123: b, 124: c, 125: d, 126: c, 127: b, 128: b, 129: b,

130. Given the choice in 1967 between a big block and a small block, which size sold more?

a.) big block   b.) small block

131. Corvette buyers did not warm up to air conditioning very fast. Still, the figures below do show a steady rise from 1963–the first year of availability–on. What year of those below has a bogus (incorrect) percentage?

a.) 1963: 1%   d.) 1966: 13%
b.) 1964: 9%   e.) 1967: 24%
c.) 1965: 10%

132. Which option shrunk to almost zero in orders by 1967?

a.) side exhausts   c.) big gas tank
b.) leather seats   d.) air conditioning

133. If you ordered your Corvette with RPO C48 in 1967, that referred to:

a.) 4-speed transmission   c.) side-mount exhausts
b.) big block engine   d.) heater-defroster delete

134. What year was the factory forced to install big block hoods on a few small block equipped cars?

a.) 1965   c.) 1967
b.) 1966   d.) 1968

135. In 1967 models, which engine option's air scoop pulled in the most air?

a.) L36   d.) L71
b.) L68   e.) L79
c.) L88

136. All of these racetrack-derived color names offered on the '67 Corvettes are from U.S. towns or U.S. tracks, save one. Can you spot the ringer?

a.) Elkhart Blue   c.) Goodwood Green
b.) Lynndale Blue   d.) Marlboro Maroon

130: b, 131: e, 132: c, 133: d, 134: c, 135: c, 136: c,

The Sting Ray Era

137. For 1967, the aluminum wheels from the factory were distinguished by:

a.) 3-bar knock-offs
b.) 2-bar knock-offs

c.) 4-bar knock-offs
d.) no knock-offs, but five lug nuts per wheel

138. Which carburetor system had the highest rated airflow?

a.) the three 2-barrels on the '67
b.) the L88's single quad

c.) the ZL1's single quad

139. For 1967, what was not a new feature?

a.) five gills for side vent
b.) rear back-up light above license plate
c.) T-tops

d.) new hood scoop design for big block

140. Which popular features available on the '67 Corvette disappeared when they brought out the '68? (Hint: more than one correct answer.)

a.) the side vent window
b.) the side pipes
c.) the humped hood on the big block

d.) the wheel trim rings

141. In the '67, where did they relocate the parking brake to?

a.) under the dashboard
b.) on the dash

c.) between the bucket seats
d.) alongside the gear shift lever

142. In 1967, what was an option introduced on the Corvette for the first time?

a.) U15 speed warning
b.) ZR4 heavy-duty suspension

c.) XL5 bronze tinted windows
d.) AR15 semi-automatic

137: d, 138: a, 139: c, 140: a & b, 141: c, 142: a,

143. The '67 was an "emergency" carry-over from 1966 because the car that became the '68 wasn't ready for introduction as a '67. Nonetheless, the '67 got a few updates so buyers wouldn't feel they were buying an "old" design. All of the changes below represent updates on the '67, except for which one?

a.) flat black rocker panels
b.) backup light above rear license plate
c.) white vinyl top for hardtop offered as an option

d.) 289 Cobra style side vents on fenders
e.) lug nut-retained alloy wheels, eliminating the knock-offs

144. Which of the following features was not part of the L88 package introduced in 1967?

a.) aluminum heads
b.) oversize valves

c.) a Holley 850 cfm carburetor
d.) an aluminum block

Bonus Question: The above photo shows what year Sting Ray?

a) 1963
b) 1964
c) 1965

d) 1966
e) 1967

THE
MAKO
SHARK
ERA

1

Bonus Question: This unusual wire mesh screen was part of an air intake that used a reverse scoop to take in cold air at the windscreen. The foam filter was lodged in the underside of the hood scoop. It was found on which following engines? (Hint: there is more than one answer.)

    a) L88   c) LT1
    b) ZL1   d) ZR2

145. In 1968, when it came to big block heads, how could you tell at a glance (when the engine is apart) if they were medium horsepower or high horsepower?

    a.) by the number of bolts on mains   c.) if pistons were fly-cut
    b.) whether oil pump pickup was   d.) by the shape of the inlet ports
         360-deg. swiveling

146. Which of the following drivers was not a National Champion in a Corvette?

    a.) Richard Thompson   c.) Don Yenko
    b.) Bob Wingate   d.) Jim Jeffords

147. What of the following engine codes listed below indicated ultra-rare L88 engines in 1969? (Hint: there is more than one answer.)

    a.) LO   d.) LX
    b.) LV   e.) LP
    c.) MR

Bonus Question: a.) L88 and b, ZL1, 145: d, 146: b, 147: a, b & c,

148. The aluminum block ZL1 was first available in what year?

a.) 1968   c.) 1970
b.) 1969   d.) 1971

149. How many ZL1s are thought to have been built for Corvettes in 1969?

a.) 2   c.) 40
b.) 20   d.) 66

150. Where were the ZL1 blocks and heads cast?

a.) Dearborn Steel Tubing,   c.) Chevrolet, Tonawanda,
Dearborn, Michigan   New York
b.) Winters Foundry,   d.) Chevrolet, Flint, Michigan
Canton, Ohio

151. The L88 was the Godzilla option for 1968. How many were sold that year?

a.) 125   c.) 425
b.) 80   d.) 1,096

152. There were two series of L88 engines. When did the second series—with changes in intake manifold and carburetor to go along with the new open chamber aluminum cylinder heads—become available?

a.) 1968   b.) 1969

153. How many L88s were automatics in 1969?

a.) 0   c.) 17
b.) 25

154. What normal feature did the L88 get in 1968 and 1969 that it lacked in 1967?

a.) a radio   c.) emergency brake
b.) a heater

155. What did the '67 L88 have as part of its braking system that other Corvettes that year didn't? Note: there's more than one answer.

a.) power brakes   c.) a proportioning valve
b.) a parking brake   d.) dual-pin front brake calipers

148: b, 149: a, 150: b, 151: b, 152: b, 153: c, 154: b, 155: c & d.

156. Back in 1969, ZL1 engine codes stamped into the block were: (Note: there's more than one answer.)

a.) ME

b.) MG

c.) MT

d.) MX

157. What "Hollywood" cowpoke bellied up to the bar in 1968 and plunked down the cash to buy two '68 L88 Corvettes to form a racing team?

a.) Clint Eastwood

b.) Dan Blocker

c.) James Garner

d.) Paul Newman

158. What was not a feature of the almighty 1969 ZL1?

a.) aluminum block

b.) aluminum heads

c.) aluminum intake manifold

d.) triple carburetion

159. By the end of 1969, how many L88s had rolled out the doors of the St. Louis factory since the engine package was first offered in 1967?

a.) 420

b.) 32

c.) 216

d.) 402

160. In a move reminiscent of the early days of the '53 Corvette (when the Corvettes were sold to VIPs and various and sundry high mucky-mucks), in 1969, three specially modified Corvette coupes were delivered to which trio of heroic Americans?

a.) SEAL team that snuck into Red China and blew up a SAM missile factory

b.) Apollo 12 astronauts

c.) three gold medal winners in the Olympics

d.) three Nobel prize winners in microbiology

161. Which Mako Shark II styling features were seen in the '68 production car? There's more than one answer.

a.) tunnel-back rear roof

b.) side exhausts

c.) retractable rear spoilers

d.) digital instrumentation

e.) none of the above

162. Which two racers named below happened to have fathers who were high GM brass (and who helped them obtain special Corvette race cars):

a.) Tony DeLorenzo

b.) Jerry Earl

c.) Dick Guldstrand

d.) Bob Bondurant

156: a & b, 157: c, 158: d, 159: c, 160: b, 161: e, 162: a & b,

163. On the changeover from 1967 to 1968, one design feature was dropped from the option list, only to reappear in 1969. What was it?

a.) side vent window
b.) hood hump for big block
c.) side-mount exhausts
d.) wheel trim rings

164. In the 1969 Corvette, what notable feature differed from the 1968 model?

a.) the outside door release
b.) the removable rear window
c.) the vacuum-operated windshield wiper cover
d.) humped hood on big block

165. What year saw a huge fall-off in convertible acceptance in the Corvette?

a.) 1966
b.) 1967
c.) 1968
d.) 1969

166. What two engines offered in 1970 were not, repeat not, available with an automatic transmission? Note: At least one choice below wasn't available that year—we listed it purposely to throw you off the trail.

a.) L48
b.) L46
c.) LT1
d.) LS6
e.) LS5

167. According to expert Karl Ludvigsen, the '68 Corvette achieved what lateral g-force reading on the skidpad?

a.) 0.74 g
b.) 0.84 g
c.) 1.0 g
d.) 1.3 g

168. Which of the following 2-seaters had a backbone-type chassis?

a.) Corvette XP-819 engineering research car
b.) De Tomaso Vallelunga
c.) Matra D'Jet
d.) De Tomaso Mangusta
e.) Corvette XP-880 engineering research car
f.) all of the above

169. Because of a long strike one year, GM thought it necessary to extend the model year into the next year's time. What model year listed below got this extra time period?

a.) 1966
b.) 1967
c.) 1968
d.) 1969

163: c, 164: a, 165: d, 166: b & c, 167: b, 168: f, 169: d,

170. In the Nicholas Cage action-thriller, *Con Air*, a pristine Sting Ray era Corvette is dropped from an airplane. What year Sting Ray was it?

a.) 1965
b.) 1966
c.) 1967
d.) 1969
e.) 1970

171. For 1968, a lot of colorful cows were needed to provide the leather. That year, interiors came in every color named below except:

a.) black
b.) red
c.) medium blue
d.) dark orange
e.) white

172. During the 1960s and 1970s, while Chevrolet was selling front-engined Corvettes, Engineering was working on mid-engined Corvette designs. One design, shown as a roadster, had a 377 cu. in. alloy block V-8 (like the Grand Sport was supposed to have gotten), and four-wheel drive, using a torque converter at each end. It would go 0 to 60 mph in a mere 2.8 seconds! What was this Larry Shinoda/Tony Lapine-designed prototype called?

a) CERV I
b) CERV II
c) XP-880
d) XP-819

173. The cylinder heads of the late 1969 L88s and ZL1s were known as:

a.) closed chamber heads
b.) open chamber heads

174. What infernal device had to be added to the L88 in 1968 and 1969 in order to meet emissions?

a.) catalytic converter
b.) a road draft tube
c.) A.I.R.

175. What color was the ZL1 block finished in (just in case you find one on a used car lot)?

a.) Chevy engine orange
b.) Chevy bow tie blue
c.) Onyx black
d.) *au natural* aluminum

176. How much did the ZL1 option package cost in 1969?

a.) $385.20
b.) $4,718.35
c.) $6,345.16
d.) $420.22

177. The LT1 was first available in:

a.) 1969

b.) 1970

c.) 1971

d.) 1975

178. The LT1 was the hot small block with a solid lifter cam, Holley carburetor and high revs, but, initially, what option wasn't available with it in the list below?

a.) AM-FM radio

b.) heater

c.) air conditioning

179. How many LT1 packages were sold in 1970 for $447.60 each?

a.) 1,287

b.) 533

c.) 423

180. When you ordered the LT1 with the ZR1 package, what did you get that you couldn't order on other Corvettes (other than big blocks with the ZR2 package)?

a.) side exhausts

b.) dual-disc clutch

c.) J56 brakes

181. The ZR1 package was first offered in:

a.) 1969

b.) 1970

c.) 1971

d.) 1972

182. What racetrack name of the ones below did Chevrolet adopt for use in 1969 as a color name when Corvettes had never raced there? Clue: we made some of the names up.

a.) LeMans Blue

b.) Tripoli Tan

c.) Carrera Panamericana Gold

d.) Monaco Orange

183. Side-mount exhausts were a popular option in 1969. How many customers ordered them?

a.) 1,006

b.) 935

c.) 1,500

d.) 4,355

184. Which of the following engines of those below did not require the K66 Transistor Ignition System in 1969? (Hint: more than one correct answer.)

a.) L46

b.) L68

c.) L88

d.) L89

e.) ZL1

177: b, 178: c, 179: a, 180: c, 181: b, 182: d, 183: d, 184: a & b,

The Mako Shark Era

185. In April 1970 Chevrolet showed the XP-882, a mid-engined Corvette, at the New York Auto Show. But they weren't the only automakers showing a mid-engined sports car powered by a made-in-U.S.A. V-8. Which of the cars listed below was not sponsored by an American automaker?

a.) AMX/III
b.) Monteverdi Hai

c.) Ford Pantera

186. The 1970 LT1 had what sort of trim on the hood to identify it?

a.) chrome lettering reading "LT-1"
b.) a foot wide stripe down the hood and the rear deck

c.) a decal between pin stripes on each side of the power dome reading "LT-1"

187. For the 1970 model year, which of the engines listed below was praised mightily in the press in advance reports but failed to materialize on the Corvette option list that year? Clue: there's more than one right answer.

a.) LS7
b.) L48

c.) L82
d.) LS6

188. OK, guys, second chance. In the 1970s, which of the engines listed below was praised mightily but failed to materialize in any year Corvette from the factory?

a.) LS7
b.) L46

c.) LS5
d.) LS6

189. If you didn't fall into the previous sand traps, you have probably figured out by now that the LS6 engine was offered in the Corvette eventually. What year and horsepower rating below represent what they listed for this monster mill?

a.) 1972/425-hp
b.) 1971/425-hp

c.) 1972/450-hp
d.) 1971/465-hp

190. In 1970 when you ordered the ZR1 package, what options did Chevrolet forbid you from ordering on your Corvette as well?

a.) air conditioning
b.) rear window defroster
c.) wheel covers
d.) radio
e.) power steering

f.) automatic transmission
g.) power windows
h.) all of the above

191. In 1971, the ZR1 option, officially called the "Special Purpose Engine Package," was still offered. GM thought slalomers would be champing at the bit to order it. They thought wrong. What were the total sales?

    a.) 256   c.) 8
    b.) 53   d.) 2

192. In 1970, John Greenwood was GT class winner at Sebring, along with what Hollywood personality as co-driver?

    a.) James Garner   c.) Jay Leno
    b.) Dick Smothers   d.) Steve McQueen

193. The Corvette Mulsanne concept car, based on a production coupe, had what unusual features at one time or another?

    a.) non-flip up headlamps   e.) side-mount exhausts
    b.) roof periscope   f.) cross-laced wheels
    c.) LT1 engine   g.) "ghost" flames
    d.) ZL1 engine   h.) all of the above

194. In what year was there a leather seat color offered called "Dark Saddle?"

    a.) 1970   c.) 1972
    b.) 1971   d.) 1973

195. The 1969 Corvette had what item added to give it more of a European flavor?

    a.) knock-off hubs   c.) fitted luggage
    b.) wood-rimmed steering wheel   d.) map pockets

196. What was the first year of the 454?

    a.) 1963   d.) 1969
    b.) 1965   e.) 1970
    c.) 1967

197. What was the compression ratio of the monster mill LS6 offered in 1971?

    a.) 12.25:1   c.) 10.0:1
    b.) 12.5:1   d.) 9:1

191: c, 192: b, 193: h, 194: d, 195: d, 196: e, 197: d,

198. In the '71 model year, you could order an automatic with what choice below?

    a.) LS6   c.) ZR1
    b.) ZR2

199. In 1971 how many big block-based "racer" ZR1 packages were sold?

    a.) 54   c.) 12
    b.) 105   d.) 0

200. What year was the last year for the pop-out rear window in the Mako Shark-inspired production Corvette?

    a.) 1969   c.) 1971
    b.) 1970   d.) 1972

201. In point of fact, exactly how many engines did the Corvette Four-Rotor have at the time of its premiere?

    a.) one   c.) four
    b.) two

202. There was a TV series in the 1960s that created a lot of interest in Corvettes because the lead characters shared one. The series was named after a famous road in America. What was the name of this television series?

    a.) Highway 1   c.) Route 66
    b.) Route 101   d.) 77 Sunset Strip

203. What's the rarest drivetrain feature you ever heard of on a Corvette? We'll give you a break and tell you the answer: a dual-disc clutch. Now, what Corvette engine of those listed below was it standard equipment on?

    a.) LT1   d.) LS6
    b.) L89   e.) ZL1
    c.) L88

198: a, 199: c, 200: d, 201: d, 202: c, 203: d.

204. Chevrolet decided Collector Editions were a good thing and subsequent higher values of Collector Editions (when kept pristine) bear out they are a good thing for buyers as well. They made one more near the end of the C4 series. Clue: It was silver. What year was it?

    a.) 1993   c.) 1996
    b.) 1994   d.) 1992

205. The XP-895 mid-engined Corvette show car was built by which automotive industry supplier?

    a.) Alcoa Aluminum   c.) ASC
    b.) Reynolds Aluminum   d.) Rohm & Haas

206. What is one of the rarest decals you'll ever find atop the air cleaner on a 1960s big block?

    a.) 325-hp   c.) 425-hp
    b.) 450-hp   d.) 435-hp

207. In the early 1970s optional weekend-racer packages, the ZR1 and ZR2, what was not a feature of the brakes?

    a.) 2-pin front caliper to hold pads   d.) heat insulators
    b.) extra front caliper supports   e.) proportioning valve
    c.) semi-metallic pads   f.) magnesium calipers

208. What was the difference in meaning between "gross" and "net" ratings that caused the big "drop" in Corvette power ratings in 1972?

    a.) "Gross" meant engines tested at sea level; "net" was at altitudes up to 1,000 ft.

    b.) "Gross" was with all accessories operating; "net" was with just the key accessories installed

    c.) "Gross" was when horsepower was measured on a laboratory dyno with unrestricted exhaust, while "net" was "as installed" with fan, production exhaust and production fuel and ignition calibrations

209. The LS6 sold as an option for what cost?

    a.) $550   d.) $1,426
    b.) $1,100   e.) $55
    c.) $1,200   f.) $1,221

210. The first year of the soft front bumper on the Corvette nose was:

    a.) 1968   c.) 1973
    b.) 1971   d.) 1984

204: c, 205: b, 206: b, 207: f, 208: c, 209: f, 210: c,

The Mako Shark Era

211. In 1971, which special performance packages listed below are correctly matched to their respective optional engines?

a.) ZR2 with LS6
b.) ZR1 with LS7
c.) Z06 with LS1
d.) ZR1 with LT1
e.) Z06 with LS6

212. In 1973, Chevrolet publicity photos showed a slotted wheel made for them by a California vendor. They then tried to recall the wheels, succeeding in getting most of them back. In what year did the same style wheels reappear, stamped with what country of origin?

a.) 1975-Bulgaria
b.) 1976-Mexico
c.) 1978-Tanzania
d.) 1982-Canada

213. You would think the last year of the big block (1974) would have resulted in a great rush of orders from big block believers. However, the actual percentage of big blocks ordered was what?

a.) 15%
b.) 25%
c.) 5%
d.) 10%

214. What was a rare Special Performance Equipment package ordered in 1973?

a.) F40
b.) F41
c.) Z07
d.) ZR2

215. What bargain-basement priced suspension package was offered in 1974?

a.) FG7
b.) FE7
c.) G7
d.) F41

216. When GM scuttled their rotary engine in the mid-1970s, the sleek silver gullwinged Four-Rotor Corvette was saved from the scrap heap by having its name magically transformed overnight to what?

a.) Aero coupe
b.) Aerovette
c.) Mulsanne
d.) GTP

217. The L82 of 1978 gave you what?

a.) 220-hp
b.) 185-hp
c.) 350-hp
d.) 190-hp

211: a & d, 212: b, 213: d, 214: c, 215: b, 216: b, 217: a,

218. In what year did the catalytic converter become standard on the Corvette?

a.) 1971   d.) 1974
b.) 1972   e.) 1975
c.) 1973

219. In 1975, what new device was added to complement the catalytic converter?

a.) braided wire for better spark   c.) ignition shielding
b.) High Energy Ignition

220. What was the alphanumeric code for the Silver Anniversary Corvette?

a.) RPO BKZ   c.) RPO 025
b.) RPO B2Z

221. What option was first offered in 1977, and then retracted from availability in a squabble between Chevrolet and its supplier over sales rights?

a.) slotted magnesium wheels   d.) AM-FM stereo radio
b.) glass roof panels   with built-in cassette.
c.) luggage rack

222. When Chevrolet had to hasten to meet the 5-mph bumper laws, for the '74 model they devised a soft plastic cover for the back of the Corvette to cover the energy absorber. What characterized the styling of the '75 version of this end cap?

a.) two-piece   b.) one-piece

223. In 1975, few noticed the Z07 package was still on the option list. The suspension and brake package included twin-pin heavy-duty brake calipers, stiffer springs front and rear, a thicker front stabilizer bar, a rear stabilizer bar and required the M21 4-speed manual. How many were ordered that year?

a.) 22   c.) 111
b.) 2   d.) 144

224. On March 15, 1977 another production milestone was reached in St. Louis. What total had they reached in Corvettes built?

a.) 300,000   c.) 500,000
b.) 250,000   d.) 1,000,000

218: e, 219: b, 220: b, 221: b, 222: b, 223: d, 224: c,

The Mako Shark Era

225. The Corvette Silver Anniversary came along in what model year? Hint: the first production Corvette was produced in 1953 (no calculators allowed!).

a.) 1976
b.) 1977
c.) 1978
d.) 1980

226. The year 1970 was Corvette's first for what?

a.) rectangular exhaust tips
b.) ZR2 package
c.) detachable rear spoiler
d.) inflatable spare

227. How many 1978 Indy Pace Car replicas did Chevrolet originally announce they were going to build?

a.) 10,000
b.) 3,000
c.) 100
d.) 2,500

228. The '78 Pace Car Replicas were heavily optioned Corvettes. They came with most of their special equipment installed, but what last but not insignificant item was left to the owner to install?

a.) the decals
b.) the wraparound chin spoiler
c.) the rear spoiler
d.) the red pin stripe

229. If you have a two-tone '81 Corvette with its original paint job, where was your car built?

a.) St. Louis, Missouri
b.) Bowling Green, Kentucky

230. In the 1982 model year, how many Collector Editions were sold?

a.) 2,500
b.) 3,250
c.) 6,759
d.) 6,502

231. What year saw Corvettes being produced simultaneously at two different GM plants in two different states?

a.) 1963
b.) 1961
c.) 1981
d.) 1984

232. In 1982, a new engine designation was proclaimed on the flanks of the Corvette. What did the name "Cross-Fire Injection" refer to?

a.) dual throttle body injection
b.) port fuel injection
c.) a high energy ignition system
d.) nitrous-oxide

225: c, 226: a, 227: d, 228: a, 229: b, 230: c, 231: c, 232: a,

233. The '78 Pace Car had a "few" options included in the package. Which option below was not included in the Pace Car's base price?

a.) A31
b.) AU3
c.) CC1
d.) C49
e.) C60
f.) D35
g.) N37
h.) QBS
i.) UA1
j.) UM2
k.) U75
l.) U81
m.) NA6
n.) YJ8
o.) ZX2

234. What color did the first "Collector Edition" come in?

a.) Gold metallic
b.) Silver Green metallic
c.) Silver blue/dark blue
d.) Silver-beige

235. As the new Corvette factory commenced operations in Bowling Green, Kentucky, in 1981, what type of paint was used?

a.) nitrocellulose lacquer
b.) 2-stage base coat-clear coat
c.) single-stage acrylic enamel
d.) single-stage acrylic lacquer

236. After a couple of limited editions, Chevrolet realized that there are those nefarious types who create "bogus" limited editions to hype the value of their used Corvette. To foil counterfeiters, what step did they take in '82 with the Collector Edition?

a.) the sixth character of the VIN identified it as a Collector Edition.
b.) started a central registry of Collector Edition buyers for future buyers of used Collector Editions to consult
c.) stamped the suspension with "CE" markings in a variety of places known only to Chevrolet
d.) etched the windshield glass with the words "Collector Edition"

237. Bill Mitchell, the second man ever to hold the post of VP in charge of styling, always liked European headlamps, i.e. French-made Marchals, Cibies or British-made Lucas. He had them installed on various Corvette prototypes. What year did the first glimmer of advanced lighting finally appear on the production Corvettes?

a.) 1975
b.) 1976
c.) 1977
d.) 1979

233: m, 234: d, 235: b, 236: a, 237: d,

238. The fastback window on the '78 that replaced the previous "tunnel-back" roof must have been popular because Chevy sold 47,667 Corvettes in 1978. What device did Chevrolet wisely install with it?

a.) a means of darkening rear glass at the touch of a button

b.) a roll-type security shade to discourage thieves from "shopping" your luggage

c.) a burglar alarm that periodically flashed a red light to discourage thieves

239. What year was the hatchback first offered in the Corvette?

a.) 1974
b.) 1976

c.) 1982
d.) 1983

240. The '82 was the Corvette's first for what transmission device?

a.) 4-plus-3 manual
b.) lock-up torque converter

c.) two-speed rear axle with control on dashboard

Bonus Question: Skirts had been popular in the early 1950s but, although they aided a car aerodynamically, they didn't really fit the character of the Corvette even if they did lower the co-efficient of drag. This prototype was inspired by pre-WWII aerodynamic speed record cars. What was it called?

a.) Speedster
b.) Astro-Vette

c.) Aerovette
d.) XP-820

238: b, 239: c, 240: b, Bonus Question: b.) Astro-Vette

THE
C4 ERA

The C4 Era

Bonus Question: This C4-based Corvette was the brainchild of which famous Corvette racer, who made a number of coupes and spyders using this body style, nearly upstaging the Corvette ZR1 in the process?

a) Bob Bondurant
b) Dick Guldstrand

c) John Greenwood
d) Reeves Callaway

241. Stung by criticism that their suspensions weren't as sophisticated as those from other countries, what foreign manufacturer did Delco tie in with in 1984 to develop a shock absorber especially for the new generation Corvette?

a.) Koni
b.) Spax

c.) Tokiko
d.) Bilstein

242. In 1984, one of the features premiered by Chevrolet on the '65 Mako Shark II show car finally made its appearance on a production Corvette. Which one below was it?

a.) clamshell hood that lifted part of fenders with hood
b.) side exhausts

c.) rear window slats that went flat at the touch of a button
d.) knock-off alloy wheels

243. In 1984 Chevrolet turned to a surprising source for their manual gearbox for the Corvette—a former drag racer gearbox maker named Doug Nash. What was his gearbox called?

a.) 7-speed
b.) 4-plus-3

c.) 4-plus-2

Bonus Question: b.) Dick Guldstrand,   241: d,   242: a,   243: b,

244. The brakes for the '84 came from:

   a.) Brembo   c.) Girlock
   b.) Speedline   d.) Lockheed

245. In 1984 option CC3 was a see-through roof. What was it made of:

   a.) laminated glass   c.) Lexan
   b.) acrylic plastic

246. What high-performance tire made its debut on the '84 Corvette?

   a.) B.F. Goodrich T/A   c.) Michelin XWX
   b.) Goodyear Eagle VR50   d.) Pirelli P-Zero

247. The drag co-efficient of the '84 was touted highly at introduction. It was:

   a.) 0.24   c.) 0.37
   b.) 0.34   d.) 0.44

248. What year was the Corvette's first for roller valve lifters?

   a.) 1956   c.) 1987
   b.) 1957   d.) 1995

249. What was the code number for the stiff suspension optional in 1984?

   a.) ZP6   c.) Z51
   b.) Z84   d.) Z52

250. How many Corvettes were built for the Corvette Challenge in 1988 by Chevrolet?

   a.) 25   c.) 56
   b.) 50   d.) 125

251. The L98 came along in what period of the 1980s?

   a.) 1985   c.) 1986
   b.) 1983   d.) 1988

252. In 1985 there was a new name for fuel injection on the Corvette. What was it?

   a.) Direct Fire Injection   c.) Ram Jet Injection
   b.) Turbojet injection   d.) Tuned Port Injection

244: c, 245: b, 246: b, 247: b, 248: c, 249: c, 250: c, 251: a, 252: d,

253. What model year did the C4 body premiere its ragtop version?

a.) 1985

b.) 1986

c.) 1988

d.) 1990 turbos

254. Back in the last millennium, the Corvette factory rolled out a number of twin-turbo prototypes but the closest they got to offering one for the public was to include a code number on the order form so the Corvette you ordered could be shipped off to a private firm in Connecticut (who would install twin turbos for you). What was the name of this Chevrolet factory-approved maestro of speed?

a.) Dick Guldstrand

b.) Reeves Callaway

c.) Roger Penske

d.) John Greenwood

255. The first few Callaway-built Twin Turbos built in 1987 used what Chevrolet block?

a.) LT1

b.) LX4

c.) LF5

d.) LO4

256. The 35th Anniversary Edition Corvette introduced April 1, 1988 at the New York Auto Show was known by what RPO number?

a.) RPO 035

b.) RPO Z01

c.) RPO Z03

d.) RPO ZR3

257. How many 35th Anniversary editions were sold by Chevrolet?

a.) 200

b.) 2,500

c.) 2,050

d.) 4,325

258. How many Callaway Speedsters were built on the C4 chassis?

a.) 5

b.) 10

c.) 12

d.) 50

259. Chevrolet built factory racing Corvettes for the public? No, we're not talking the Grand Sports of 1963. In 1988-1989, Chevrolet actually built short runs of Corvettes for SCCA competitors with sealed engines to prevent teams from modifying them. The goal was to have all the engines be of equal power so the series would be a true contest of driving talent alone. What was this series called?

a.) World Challenge

b.) Pro Fab Series

c.) Corvette Superstock Series

d.) Corvette Challenge Series

253: b, 254: b, 255: c, 256: b, 257: c, 258: c, 259: d.

260. The following are for sales of the Callaway Twin Turbo except for one ringer. Which one of the figures below is a bogus number?

a.) 1987 = 181
b.) 1988 = 124
c.) 1989 = 188
d.) 1990 = 58
e.) 1991 = 62

261. Most Corvette fans will say the King Kong of C4 generation Corvettes was the 4-cam ZR1. Others favor the Callaway Twin Turbo. If you look at the year 1990, when the ZR1 was introduced, which one put the other to shame on torque?

a.) Callaway Twin Turbo
b.) Corvette ZR1

262. The Corvettes in the Corvette Challenge Series ran different wheels than the Corvettes sold in the showrooms. Who was the wheel manufacturer?

a.) BBS
b.) Campagnolo
c.) Speedline
d.) Dymag

263. In 1989, the Corvette got a 6-speed gearbox as a no-cost option. It was made by what German supplier?

a.) Getrag
b.) ZF
c.) Mercedes
d.) Porsche

264. In 1989 what was the purpose of the 6-speed manual ZF's "bypass" feature?

a.) to help you get to 6th gear that much faster
b.) to be able to operate the 6-speed more like an automatic by reducing the number of gears to row through
c.) to force you to "short shift" from 1st to 4th in order to meet CAFE standards

265. For the 1989 model year, Chevrolet built how many "production" ZR1 Corvettes? (Warning: trick question here...)

a.) 0
b.) 80-100
c.) 25
d.) 56

260: c, 261: a, 262: d, 263: b, 264: c, 265: b.

266. In 1989, the tri-mode suspension was only available on coupes with a manual gearbox and Z51 handling package. What was the option code number for the variable choice Selective Ride and Handling?

a.) AX3
b.) FX3
c.) EX3
d.) EO3

267. The Lotus-designed 4-cam Corvette engine was built for Chevy by what outside supplier?

a.) Lotus
b.) Lamborghini
c.) Mercury Marine
d.) Evinrude

268. In 1990 there was another racing series for Corvettes, which Chevrolet again built cars for. In this one you could build the engine yourself or buy it prepared from Chevrolet. What was this new series called?

a.) Popular Challange
b.) Motor Trend Challenge
c.) World Challenge
d.) Earth Challenge

269. The new Thousand Oaks, California design studio of GM, established in order to get that "California look" into GM cars, came up with a startling deep purple front-engined show car in 1992 that was a smaller design than the later production C5 (introduced in 1997) turned out to be. But it had its influence nonetheless. What was this one-off prototype called?

a.) CERV III
b.) Stingray III
c.) CERV IV
d.) Aerovette

270. The LT5 shared what with the L98?

a.) bore centers
b.) pistons
c.) cam profile
d.) throttle body

271. In 1992, the revised small block pushrod engine had an unusual feature. What was it?

a.) alloy block
b.) four cams
c.) Eaton supercharger
d.) reverse flow cooling

272. In 1992, what was unusual about the Goodyear GS-C that were standard equipment on the Corvette?

a.) they glowed in the dark
b.) they were smooth faced, like "cheater" slicks
c.) they had an asymmetrical tread pattern
d.) they had the word "Corvette" molded into them

273. How wide were the rear wheels on the ZR1?

a.) 9.5 inches
b.) 10 inches
c.) 11 inches
d.) 11.5 inches

274. The official nomenclature for the four cam engine offered in the Corvette was:

a.) ZR1
b.) LT5
c.) CR5
d.) LT4

275. In 1986, in a real departure, Chevrolet agreed to run off a special limited edition of fifty Corvettes to honor a specific dealer. This Commemorative Edition had its own special two-tone paint job. What dealership was so honored?

a.) Harry Mann Chevrolet
b.) Nickey Chevrolet
c.) Dana Chevrolet
d.) Malcolm Konner Chevrolet

276. Chevrolet used Lotus to test experimental features on their mid-engined Corvette Indy prototype. What was the "secret weapon" Lotus fitted their prototype with—one that GM thought would change auto history?

a.) Active Suspension
b.) JATO assist
c.) Rajo dual range rear axle
d.) infra-red night vision
e.) Stirling engine
f.) die-cast chassis

277. In 1992, a new small block was introduced, recalling the name of a great engine in the Corvette's past. What was it called?

a.) L79
b.) LT1
c.) LT4
d.) L76

278. In the 1980s what was the marketing name chosen for the new "distributorless" engine in the Corvette?

a.) Turbo-Jet
b.) Turbo-Fire
c.) Astro-Fire
d.) Direct-Fire

279. It is a little known fact that several LT5-powered convertibles were built for testing purposes, but Chevrolet decided the convertible lost too much rigidity to be able to handle the increased power and there was worry the top would be ripped off by the wind blast at 160 mph. Nonetheless, one GM official was presented with a custom-styled 4-cam Corvette convertible as a personal gift. Who was that?

a.) Dave McLellan
b.) Dave Hill
c.) Zora Arkus-Duntov
d.) Don Runkle

280. In 1992 the new standard Traction Control System came from:

a.) Bosch
b.) Girling
c.) Lockheed
d.) Delco

281. The DOHC LT5, in its first incarnation, produced how much more horsepower than the pushrod L98?

a.) 20
b.) 75
c.) 125-130
d.) 240

282. In addition to the Indy pace cars, where Corvettes have been the choice on several occasions, Chevrolet co-operated with an auto industry supplier to build two pace cars for another racing series, this during the C4 production. What was the name of the outside supplier?

a.) Firestone
b.) Libby-Owens-Ford
c.) PPG
d.) Goodyear

283. The ZR1 had, of course, its own special engine, its wider wheels and tires, and its own unique rear styling for one year, but what was unusual about the glass?

a.) it went dark on the sides and rear at the touch of a button
b.) it could "breathe"
c.) it had a "solar" windscreen that cut down on the heat load

278: d, 279: d, 280: a, 281: c, 282: c, 283: c,

284. ZR1s came with a key-operated switch, which, if activated by the owner, cut the power output in the car to 250-hp. Whose enthusiasm was this fiendish device designed to dampen?

a.) car thieves
b.) valets
c.) wives driving their husband's car

285. In 1993, the old PASS key system was replaced by the:

a.) Kohler push button
b.) Schlage Entry system
c.) Active Key Entry system
d.) Passive Keyless Entry (PKE)

286. How many of the higher horsepower second-generation ZR1s were sold once they could brag about having 405-hp?

a.) 100
b.) 1,344
c.) 502
d.) 3,044

287. On July 2, 1992, in Bowling Green, Kentucky, a white Corvette roadster with red interior rolled down the assembly line. It marked what milestone in the number of Corvettes built?

a.) 750,000
b.) 1,250,000
c.) 1,500,000
d.) 1,000,000

288. The ZR1 had a lot of power when it was introduced. What was one of Chevy's hot rodders' tricks to get the additional horses in the second generation?

a.) chop and channel
b.) nose and deck
c.) hand porting
d.) tuck and roll

289. In 1992, a new Corvette chief engineer was named. Can you pick him out of this list of famous Corvette personalities?

a.) Zora Arkus-Duntov
b.) Joe Pike
c.) Jerry Palmer
d.) Dave Hill
e.) Dave McLellan

290. The 1993 40th Anniversary (RPO Z25) package-equipped Corvettes are collector's items all by themselves. If you have access to a time machine, what option should you go back in time and order with your 40th Anniversary to make sure it's even more of a "keeper?"

a.) AC3
b.) FX3
c.) ZR1
d.) Z25

284: b, 285: d, 286: b, 287: d, 288: c, 289: d, 290: c.

291. On the 1996 Grand Sport RPO Z16 package, what was the width of the rear wheels on the convertible only?

a.) 9 inches   c.) 10.5 inches
b.) 11 inches   d.) 9.5 inches

292. Due to painting difficulties, what color turned out to be extremely rare in the 1994 Corvette?

a.) Admiral Blue   c.) Torch Red
b.) Copper Metallic   d.) Polo Green Metallic

293. When did the National Corvette Museum open to the public in Bowling Green, Kentucky?

a.) June 1, 1957   c.) Sept. 2, 1994
b.) June 1, 1981   d.) Sept. 2, 1995

294. In 1996 the LT4 optional engine had several features that made it more desirable than the LT1. Which feature listed below was not part of the LT4 package in 1996?

a.) 330-hp   d.) Crane roller rackers
b.) 10.8 compression   e.) automatic transmission
c.) new aluminum head design   f.) revised cam profile

(Photo courtesy Corvette Mike Vietro)

Bonus Question: Which Corvette race car of the 1960s did this '90s Corvette production car borrow the name and color scheme (blue with white stripe) of?

a) Z06   c) SS
b) Grand Sport   d) SR2

291: c, 292: b, 293: c, 294: e, Bonus Question: b.) Grand Sport

THE
C5 ERA

(Photo courtesy Corvette Mike Vietro)

Bonus Question: What controversial color were the wheels on the Indy Pace car of 1988?

a) white

b) silver

c) yellow

d) chartreuse

295. What kind of spare tire did the C5 have when it was introduced in 1997?

a.) narrow rim alloy wheel, inflatable spare

b.) narrow rim steel wheel, inflatable spare

c.) full width aluminum-spoked rim carrying front tire size

d.) none

296. The first prototype shown of the mid-engined Corvette Indy show car, a silver targa, had a twin turbo engine made in Europe by:

a.) Coventry Climax

b.) Cosworth

c.) Ilmor

d.) BRM

297. What unusual component (for a modern car) was used in the C5 Corvette?

a.) "Dagmar" front bumpers

b.) Tom Corbett space cadet rocket ship-style dashboard

c.) Balsa wood core in the floorboards

d.) Captain Midnight Secret Decoder

Bonus Question :c.) yellow, 295: d, 296: c, 297: c,

298. In the case of the '98 Indianapolis 500 pace car, the car came fairly "loaded" ("optioned out"). What were some remaining options that you still had to pay extra for if you wanted them on your Pace Car replica?

a.) front license plate holder
b.) 12-disc CD changer
c.) body side moldings
d.) magnesium wheels
e.) all of the above

299. In 1998, how many production Pace Car replicas were made?

a.) 1,088
b.) 500
c.) 1,163
d.) 2,500

300. New colors in 2000 included: (Clue: more than one answer.)

a.) Gunmetal Gray
b.) Quicksilver Metallic
c.) Dark Bowling Green
d.) Millennium Yellow

Bonus Question: What year marked the introduction of the Z06 in the C5 series?

a) 1997
b) 1998
c) 1999
d) 2000
e) 2001

298: e; 299: c; 300: c & d, Bonus Question: 2001

The
Inside
Scoop
(Expanded Answers)

The Boulevardier Years

1. **The word "Corvette" referred to a naval fighting ship somewhat smaller than a destroyer. It was extensively used by the Canadian Navy to escort ships during WWII and the term is still used by some Navies (such as Kuwait Navy) today.**

   The word was chosen by Chevrolet PR man Myron Scott after an internal contest to search for the right name for Chevy's new sports car. Interestingly, one of the early Motorama show cars, a fastback coupe with the Corvette body, was called the Corvair, a name that they picked up later for their rear-engined air-cooled passenger car.

2. **As GM was thinking of making their own sports car, the Nash-Healey, Cunningham, and Kaiser-Darrin 2-seater sports cars were already being sold in America.**

   The Nash-Healey was conceived when a Nash official met Donald Healey on a ship during an Atlantic crossing. The chassis was made in America, bodywork first in England, then later in Italy. The engine was Nash. Cunningham built chassis in Florida, installed Chrysler engines and had his cars bodied in Italy. Kaiser-Darrin used a "Dutch" Darrin design for an all made-in-U.S.A. fiberglass-bodied car. The California-made Chevy-powered Scarab didn't come until the late 1950s. It was the brainchild of Lance Reventlow, whose mother had a 500-million-dollar fortune. Only a handful of Scarabs were made (for racing only), but they scared the Ferraris for awhile.

3. **A Signal Seeking radio and heater were mandatory "options" on the '53 Corvette.**

   The radio cost $145.15 and the heater $91.40, bringing the total price to $3,734.55.

4. **Corvettes were in short supply in 1953 so GM decided to sell them only to the rich and famous to extract publicity value. One American family that got three of them was the DuPonts.**

   Of course the fact that the DuPonts owned a significant interest in GM had nothing to do with it. The Corvettes were reportedly the 3rd, 4th and 5th off the line. Chevrolet's VIP marketing policy did little to help public awareness of the new kid on the block.

5. **The Blue Flame six was heavier than the V-8 Corvette engine in 1955.**

   It was heavier by 40 lbs but the V-8 had 10 lbs of extra equipment so the difference was really 30 lbs.

6. **For the '53 Corvette there were 46 separate body pieces.**
Chevrolet staged publicity photos showing all the body pieces laid out. As the years went on, Corvette bodies were made of many more parts.

7. **If you are doing a body-off restoration on your '53-'55 Corvette, you might need more than four buddies to lift the body off the frame. It weighed 411 lbs.**
This was still lightweight compared to steel bodies of the time.

8. **The Corvette originally came with only one interior color—red. By 1954, beige was a second interior color added. Beige was only available with Pennant Blue.**
Beige didn't help sales, but there is a rumor they tried an even wilder solution: green exterior with yellow interior. So far, such a color combination is undocumented.

9. **A.O. Smith manufactured the frame for the '53 Corvette.**
The plant was in Milwaukee. Frames were welded, painted and shipped first to Flint, then St. Louis when they switched plants for the '54 models.

10. **Molded Fiber Glass Co. was the supplier of fiberglass body parts for Chevrolet in 1953.**
They made their first money by making boats. The owner, a man named Morrison, set up a new company in order to supply Chevrolet. Later on, Owens-Corning supplied the fiberglass material but did not assemble the bodies. Chevy built a '52 Club Coupe of glass-reinforced plastic to test the material. They accidentally rolled it and when the driver emerged with only minor injuries, they decided they liked the material.

11. **The radio antenna on the '53 Corvettes was found in an unusual place—the rear deck lid.**
The antenna was a wire mesh molded into the rear deck lid.

12. **A plastic body and plastic side curtains, two features of the '53 Corvette, were also found on the first production Dodge Viper more than 30 years later.**
Chrysler was in a hurry to get their Corvette competitor, the Viper, to market. They figured they could save time by working out solutions for the side windows and door locks later, which is exactly what Chevrolet figured in 1953. Ironically, echoing Corvette history, the Viper production car also sprang nearly complete from a popular show car.

13. Harley Earl was the true father of the Corvette.

Although as time went on Zora Arkus-Duntov was hailed as the "father of the Corvette," in truth the Corvette was one of half a dozen two-seater sporty show cars that Earl ordered built for his traveling road shows called "Motoramas." Maurice Olley was the engineer who designed the frame, and Bob McLean oversaw the styling. Duntov came along after it had already been selected for production and turned their boulevardier into a rip-roaring sports car. So technically Duntov is the "godfather" of the Corvette.

14. Early in Corvette history, in 1954, there were many leftover, unsold Corvettes.

Estimates are as many as 1,400 out of 3,640 built were left unsold. It could have been the news of a V-8 coming for 1955 that soured 1954 sales. Also, the public didn't know how to perceive the Corvette. It wasn't considered a sports car until it began to be raced and that wasn't until 1956.

15. The Corvette enjoyed two years of being America's only domestic sports car, but then the Blue Oval folks over in Dearborn spoiled that by introducing the 2-seat Thunderbird in 1955. The first year they both were on the market, the Thunderbird outsold the Corvette.

Ford's Thunderbird had roll-up windows and a V-8 in every car. It whomped the Corvette, selling 16,155 units compared to the Corvette's 700.

Zora Targets the 300SL

16. Zora Arkus-Duntov came on board at GM in May 1953.

Duntov wrote Ed Cole, Chevrolet's chief engineer, before he worked for GM, saying he would like to work on the then newly introduced Corvette. He was hired to work on other projects but gravitated to the Corvette Development Group because his racing background was regarded as an asset.

17. In 1955, when Chevy began to offer the V-8 in the Corvette, they kept the six-cylinder six-volt.

The poor ol' six was left with its inadequate 6-volt electrical system, so Chevy was building two versions of the Corvette electrical system on the same assembly line simultaneously. McCullough, an aftermarket firm, offered a supercharger for the Corvette, but it was not a dealer-orderable option. Fuel injection didn't come until 1957.

18. In 1957, Chevrolet fielded a special Corvette in the Sebring 12-hour race called the Corvette SS. It cost over one million dollars to build.

The "SS" could have stood for "Super Sport," a name they tried earlier on a less ambitious Corvette show car based on a stock production car. The tube-framed racer unabashedly copied the Mercedes 300SL tubular space frame (GM had their own gullwing 300SL) and used a lightweight magnesium body painted blue. The white test "mule" used a fiberglass body. The beautiful blue SS lasted only 23 laps into the race, DNF-ing after the rubber suspension bushings failed, rendering the car undrivable at speed. The mule chassis was later to re-emerge in combat under the body of the Stingray Special.

19. When you ordered "dual quads" on a Corvette, you received twin 4-barrel carburetors.

In the slang of the time, rodders also called twin 4-barrels "twin pots" or "two fours." They were notoriously hard to tune and delivered poor mid-range performance.

20. Famous cowboy hat-wearing mechanic Smokey Yunick did the prep work on the three '56 factory-owned Corvette beach racers that ran on the packed sands of Daytona Beach, Florida.

On at least one of the Corvettes, Smokey installed his own cool air induction system. He became a favorite mechanic for various Chevrolet racing efforts in the next decade. The slogan painted on his shop exterior was "The Best Damn Garage in Town." The others mentioned are all race drivers, except for Balchowsky who was a driver and a mechanic.

21. The year 1956 saw the biggest year-to-year sales increase in Corvettes during the twentieth century.

Sales went from 700 in 1955 to 3,467 in 1956. The public must have liked the new styling on the nose and tail, though, and few suspected that it was the same old 1953-1955 bodyshell underneath the cosmetic face-lifts. Other years saw a near doubling in Corvette sales but 1956 remains one of the biggest year-to-year sales increases recorded in Corvette history.

22. The '57 "Airbox" cars relocated the tach atop the steering column.

The tach was easier to see on the steering column than on the dash. The hole left when it was moved was covered with the Corvette circular emblem normally found on the trunk. Some racers may have bought the airbox from the Chevrolet Parts Dept. and thus their cars might look authentic at first glance, but not if they didn't also duplicate the special brakes with finned drums and vented backing plates.

23. The Corvette heavy-duty racing package of 1957 was coded RPO 684.

Chevrolet was getting ready to back factory teams at Sebring in 1957. They needed to have a raft of racing goodies available to the public so they could run them on the race cars and still have the race cars classified as production cars (rather than modified, where they would be less competitive). The option, which consisted of heavy-duty brakes and heavy-duty suspension parts, was available around April 1957. It sold for $780.10.

24. In 1957, the optional wide wheels, RPO 276, were 5.5 inches.

These allowed you to run 7.10 tires, which had a bigger footprint. These wheels came with "dog dish" hubcaps, the little ones less prone to fall off during cornering than the full-size wheel covers. Roughly 51 sets were sold at $15.10, according to the NCRS Spec. Guide. They only became available about April 1957.

25. "Metallics" referred to HD metallic brake linings.

The HD metallic brake linings were needed because the base organic linings overheated and faded on the racetrack. Drums were finned on this option for cooling as well. The metallics didn't work well when cold.

26. In the mid-1950s, GM figured they needed to reach a production target of 10,000 in order for the Corvette to make a profit.

GM gamely kept the money-losing Corvette in production for a decade before they began to see a profit. By the 1980s, their policy was to drop a car model in less than five years if it wasn't selling according to projections. The Allante, Reatta, and Fiero were all victims of this policy.

27. Zora Arkus-Duntov and his brother, Yura, first became known to American hot rodders when they developed a conversion head for the flathead Ford called "Ardun."

They didn't make money on it, but it brought the brothers to the attention of American enthusiasts.

28. Comparing 1956 and 1957, the big sales winner was the year 1957.

The figures were 3,467 in 1956 and 6,339 in 1957.

29. In 1957, if you ordered fuel injection, you wanted to let everyone know you had Chevy's new secret weapon. But no emblem proclaiming fuel injection was located on the nose of the car, only the side coves and trunk lid.

There were probably more sales of Part No. 37422212—the script reading "Fuel Injection," than there were fuel-injected cars in 1957. Nobody knew if you had it or not until you put the pedal to the metal. One Corvette expert, Jim Gessner, says the first two proto-types did claim "Fuel Injection" on the nose as well.

30. The paint color choice ordered on the fewest '57 Corvettes was Inca Silver.

It was a late offering, and was a sort of warm-up for 1958. This was the only '57 color that was acrylic lacquer ("Lucite") instead of "Duco" nitrocellulose lacquer. Only 65 of the 6,339 '57s made came in this dark gray tone.

31. Old Corvette dream cars never die, they just reappear in new guises. Jim Jeffords, sponsored by Nickey Chevrolet of Chicago, raced Jerry Earl's SR2 in SCCA B-Production racing, winning a national title in the late 1950s. He named the car after a popular song. The title of the forgettable ditty was "The Purple People Eater."

Jeffords, affiliated with Nickey Chevrolet, happened to try to buy the car just at the time GM was going through one of its anti-racing moods and dispensing of race cars. He got lucky, getting a genuine GM prototype. It was later replaced by a normal-bodied Corvette carrying the same name. "Purple People Eater" was a comedy record, taking off on the public's fascination for flying saucers, and the "purple people eaters" that piloted them.

32. Bill Mitchell, VP in charge of styling at GM, and Harley Earl, his former boss, both shared passions for Panama hats, side exhausts, aircraft-inspired gauges, superchargers, and tailfins, but Mitchell alone liked motorcycles.

Mitchell, toward the end of his career, siphoned off some designers to design motorcycle cafe racer bodywork in his secret underground studio, much to the annoyance of GM bean counters, who saw no profit for GM in this.

33. The side coves in the '56 were first previewed on the GM-built Biscayne show car and LaSalle II show cars.

Both cars made the rounds of auto shows in 1955. Bill Mitchell may have taken the idea off an Italian one-off car seen on one of his European trips. Interestingly, one of the '55 Corvette racers run by Chevrolet on the packed sands at Daytona Beach had painted "coves" without the inset, revealing Chevrolet was already planning con-trasting coves for the next model year.

34. GM unveiled several 2-seater show cars at their Motorama road shows in the mid-1950s, including the LeSabre, Cadillac LeMans, Buick Wildcat II, Chevrolet Corvette, and Oldsmobile F88.

Although GM showed a variety of 2-seaters, poor sales of the Corvette in 1954 killed off the idea of offering a 2-seater sporty car from each Division. There was a 4-seater show car called the Corvette Impala, which had grille teeth like the production Corvette and the side coves like the '56 Corvette (though they pointed in the opposite direction) but it had no other family resemblance. Perhaps at the time Chevrolet was thinking of spawning a whole "Corvette family."

35. RPO 275 5.5-inch wide wheels, RPO 678 Positraction (4.11 ratio), RPO 685 4-speed transmission, and RPO 684 HD racing suspension and brakes are some of the options that were available with the "airbox" '57 Corvettes.

There were bullet-shaped covers for the front headlamps on Bill Mitchell's SR2 and a couple of other race Corvettes but they were never on any option list.

36. The '56 and '57 Corvettes' upholstery had a pattern that looked like the pattern created by a waffle iron.

The 1958 interior went more space-age and the waffle pattern, fortunately, was dropped.

37. The kind of paint used on the '58 Corvette was acrylic lacquer.

GM needed a paint that was fast drying and easy to repair. Acrylic lacquer was a more durable version of the old-fashioned nitrocellulose lacquer. Both dry quickly and are easy to spot repair but require buffing to bring out the gloss.

38. In 1956, the good news was that you got the removable top (RPO 419) at no extra cost if you didn't want the soft-top. If you decided you also wanted the soft-top, you had to pay an additional $215.20.

A brave 629 souls ordered the hardtop only, figuring they could lift it off on sunny days. After lifting it a few times, most probably regretted they hadn't ordered the soft-top as well.

39. The Wonder Bar radio of 1956 used transistors, at that time earthshaking, state-of-the-art, cutting-edge technology.

Transistors were pretty new then. Short wave was not offered by GM but foreign automakers in Europe offered car radios that would receive short wave. Citizen's band wasn't in vogue yet.

40. The Corvette Super Sport show car made only a brief appearance in auto shows, slipped into private hands, and then disappeared from public view for more than 40 years.

The Corvette Super Sport was an imitation SR2 "clone" similar to the Harlow Curtice "let's pretend" SR2 in that it had some SR2 accoutrements but was not a full SR2. It was white with a normal 1956-1957 grille, but had a cockpit with two racing "bubble" windscreens, and a racing stripe running nose to tail over the hood and down the trunk. The SR2 side coves (with brushed metal inserts) were there. But the wheels were ordinary wheel covers, not the Halibrand mags of the race cars. Tires were narrow whitewalls. The car is reported to have been stolen, crashed into either a tree or a train (take your choice of rumors) and still be in storage in Michigan as we go to press. Noland Adams pictures it in his book, *Corvette: American Legend Series*, which covers the '56 Corvette.

41. Prince Bertil of Sweden bought a Corvette in 1956 with the "trunk irons" zooming up the trunk lid like the '58 Corvette.

Usually European princes ordered the latest Ferrari or Maserati, but after Prince Bertil was given a tour of GM Styling by Harley Earl, he took a liking to a Corvette prototype featuring the not-yet-featured trunk trim. Noland Adams, the Corvette historian, says the prototype body was installed on a '56 Corvette chassis for him. Years later, in Sweden, it was damaged in an accident, its body rebuilt with stock parts, and it was used by a commoner for drag racing. Happily, it is now reported to be the subject of a restoration to original one-off restoration.

42. RPO 579E makes a '57 Corvette very valuable if you can document that it's original. RPO 579E refers to the fresh air intake and mechanical tachometer on the steering column.

Michael Antonick, Corvette historian, says 43 "airbox" cars were built. Not many, but it was a $726.30 option, about $250 more than the 283 engine without the airbox. Even if it is missing the airbox today, if the presence of holes in the right place indicate it was an airbox car originally, that could make even a wreck valuable enough to restore.

43. Inventor of the Corvette's fuel injection system was John Dolza.

The GM engineer developed it in 1955 whereupon Duntov was assigned to work with him on it, so it is safe to assume Duntov brought the system to the Corvette. Duntov, a real trooper, worked on the project even though at the time he had a broken back from a racing accident.

44. Pontiac offered Ram Jet fuel injection in 1957. Their system differed in the air cleaner.

On the Corvette the air cleaner was tilted sideways, open-sided and was topped with chrome metal, where on the Pontiac Bonneville the air cleaner was hidden in a black housing.

45. Topaz blue was not an exterior color choice in 1957.

The blue offered on that year's Corvette was Arctic Blue. There were seven colors in all on the 1957 color chart, including Polo White and Onyx Black.

46. In 1960, when you ordered the Duntov-cammed 270-bhp twin carburetor engine, the tachometer came redlined at 6,500 rpm.

Hydraulic lifter engines weren't so adventurous. They were redlined at 5,300 rpm.

47. In 1956, RPO 440 referred to cars with two-tone paint.

The second tone was applied only to the cove area. Six colors were available with the two-tone treatment, which cost under $20.00.

48. Corvettes were occasionally re-bodied in Italy. By the late 1990s, some of the carrozzerias (CA-ROTZ-ZOH-RHEE-UH) or coachbuilders had bodied at least one Corvette. They were Scaglietti, Vignale, Bertone, and Pininfarina.

Gordon Kelly had one done by Vignale in 1960; a Road & Track cover car. In 1958, three were built by Sergio Scaglietti for Gary Laughlin, who was part of a Texan triumvirate, including Jim Hall and Carroll Shelby, who were thinking of setting up a business importing Italian-bodied Corvettes. But, perhaps fearing they would succeed, GM cut them off from Corvette chassis after three cars. Pininfarina built a show car on a 1963 Corvette chassis hoping to get a GM contract. They had already bodied Cadillac Brougham limousines for GM. Pininfarina later won a contract from GM Design for building the one-off Two-Rotor Corvette, but it was built to a GM design. In the 1990s, Bertone designed and built two one-off Corvettes, one front-engined and one mid-engined. Chevy didn't buy either one.

49. According to noted Corvette historian Noland Adams, the 24-gallon gas tank option was offered in 1957 to Corvette racers from the factory though not listed on any option lists.

In Vol. 1 of his *Corvette Restoration and Technical Guide*, Corvette historian Noland Adams says seven of the tanks were installed on Corvettes in 1957 in St. Louis, despite the option not being listed.

Halibrands were only fitted on the factory SR racers. Corvette's first lightweight body came in the 1963 Grand Sport racers and the first aluminum engine block in a production Corvette came in the 1969 ZL1.

50. The '59 Corvette basically used the 1958 body style, though the trunk irons zooming up the trunk lid had disappeared. A storage bin under the grab bar was added to the interior.
During this period, the Corvette was going in two directions—luxury, and toward more performance, though GM still hadn't decided precisely what their target market was.

51. The T-shaped reverse lock-out handle just below the knob on the gearshift first appeared in 1959.
The idea was that you had to pull up on the T-handle before you could go into reverse to prevent accidental reverse engagement.

52. Fuel injection of the original Rochester Ram Jet type had its highs and lows in popularity from 1957 through 1965.
Fuel injection, in its first incarnation, was dropped when the model year 1965 came to a close. It came back over a decade later in digital electronic form.

53. The option RPO 686, available in 1959, referred to metallic brake linings.
These Delco-Moraine linings were chosen because of a metallic content for durability. They used the base brake drum, but it was polished with a finer finish. They took a little time to warm up, but were a bargain at $26.90.

54. American millionaire Briggs Swift Cunningham took a team of Corvettes to race at the 24 Hours of LeMans in France in June 1960.
Ten years earlier, ex-America's Cup yachtsman Cunningham chose Cadillacs to race at LeMans. His middle name was not a description of his love for racing—his family money came from the Swift meat-packing firm. A humorous note is that his Team Captain, John Fitch, was able to ship the team's three Corvettes via ocean liner to Europe as "excess baggage."

55. The '59 Corvette's coves were available in the colors Inca Silver and Snowcrest White.
According to historian Michael Antonick, 2,931 '59 Corvettes were ordered with the two-tone option out of 9,670 made.

56. **In 1959, a turquoise colored soft-top was offered—a color that never reappeared in the "solid axle days."**
This may have been the last gasp of the popularity of turquoise as a color. It was available with Snowcrest White and Crown Sapphire exteriors.

The Duck-Tail Era

57. **The contrasting coves cost $16.15 in 1961.**
If you didn't order this option, you got a body color cove.

58. **1961 was the last year for wide whitewalls on the Corvette.**
Back in the 1940s and 1950s, "wide whites" were considered the ultimate in luxury, but eventually it was thought they made a car look too dowdy. Besides, they required a lot of upkeep to keep clean.

59. **For many years chrome grilles were the standard. Then suddenly Chevrolet discovered anodizing in gold blacking out grilles in 1962.**
The '62 Corvette was only the second of a "two-year model." They didn't want to tool up for a cosmetic change so switching to a black grille was one way to do a quick update. There is some recent evidence that a gold anodized grille was also available in 1962 and that even the black grille may have been black over the anodizing.

60. **In 1962, the Corvette engine went from 283 cu. in. to 327 cu. in.**
In this form, it achieved most of its successes. It was tougher than the Ford 289 Shelby was using, and wound higher.

61. **In 1961, the Corvette passed the "break-even point" and started making a profit.**
In truth the '61 was really the same chassis and body as the '53. That's how long it took to cover initial tooling costs.

62. **1962 was the last year for the competition style 3-spoke aluminum steering wheel with drilled spokes that had been around since 1956.**
The '63 had aluminum spokes but with long elongated slots instead of lightening holes. According to Corvette restorer Mike Scott, there was an interesting steering wheel called the Service Replacement Wheel, which had the wrong surface finish on the metal and is a rare item.

63. **In 1962, when you ordered the Special High Performance 340 or 360-hp fuel injected engine, the tachometer redline moved up to 6,500 rpm.**

Also, according to historian Michael Antonick, all tachometers were distributor-driven in 1962 whereas previously carburetor engines' tachometers were driven off the generator.

64. **The small aluminum keg placed horizontally under the hood of some '61 Corvettes was a remote expansion tank needed in those Corvettes equipped with the new aluminum cross-flow radiator.**
When coolant gets hot, it has to go someplace. The expansion tank was it. Some radiators had built-in expansion tanks. The new aluminum cross-flow radiator didn't so the remote tank had to be added. In 1962 all the Corvettes got the keg-like expansion tank.

65. **In 1962, the side view of the Corvette was enhanced by rocker panel molding made of ribbed aluminum.**
Some felt the new rocker panel moldings made the car look lighter. Others don't care for it.

66. **When Chevrolet went to the duck-tail styling on the rear of the '61, luggage space was increased by 20 percent.**
The design was previewed in Mitchell's XP-700 show car.

67. **In 1962, the heater/defroster option became standard, making the Corvette more civilized.**
You could delete this feature by ordering code RPO 610, which designated "export." But it was really for racing.

68. **Corvettes in 1961 were the last to have contrasting coves.**
The removal of chrome trim from the coves made it more difficult to offer two-tone. No loss—the two-tone craze of the 1950s was getting old by then.

69. **Cosmetic changes on '62 Corvettes did not include a black chrome shift lever on manual. It was a white ball on the manual.**
The method of black chroming hadn't been discovered by GM yet.

70. **Drivers Don Yenko and Frank Dominianni were B-production competitors in Corvettes in 1962.**
Lance Reventlow and Roger Penske were also racers then, but not necessarily in Corvettes. Reventlow was a wealthy playboy whose Corvette-powered Scarabs scared the Ferraris for a while. Penske raced until the mid-1960s but made his racing name in his own Xerex Special and later the Corvette Grand Sport. The new '62 with the 327 was classified as A-production, but Yenko and Dominianni continued to race earlier 283s in B-Production.

71. Although duck-tails are pretty similar in 1961 and 1962, the color blue was dropped from the interior in 1962.

Blue sold the poorest in 1961 so Chevy dropped it.

The Sting Ray Era

72. The 1963 model year saw a jump in sales of almost 50% from the year before.

The popularity of the '63 might be explained due to it being the first year of the Stingray race car-inspired body style. Sales went from 14, 531 in 1962 to 21,513 in 1963, an increase of 48 percent.

73. The car shown by GM today as the "Mako Shark I" show car was originally known as the "Shark."

The XP-755 "Shark" show car made its debut at Wisconsin's Road America track in 1961 as the "Shark." The reason for the confusion is that some PR man, noting years later that there was a Mako Shark II, thought that there should logically be a Mako Shark I and had the original Shark renamed after it was mildly restyled. Go figure!

74. "Bunkie" Knudsen, a GM executive who liked racing, planned to build 125 Grand Sport coupes for the 1963 racing season.

Higher GM brass found out about the secret program and cancelled it, invoking the fact that GM had signed the 1957 Automobile Manufacturer's Association (AMA) resolution to not promote racing. The actual numbers of GS coupes completed were a mere five. According to FIA rules at the time, a minimum of 100 would have had to have been built in order for the Grand Sport to qualify as a production sports car. That's why Porsche built over 100 904GTS models in 1964.

75. The original Grand Sport race cars of 1963 were planned to have engines displacing 377 cu. in.

The engines were not immediately provided with the cars when the cars were smuggled out to racers. Eventually, racers did get the 377-inchers, but the engines lacked the twin plug hemi-head that the original prototype 550-hp engine had.

76. John Fitch and Larry Shinoda both spent a portion of WWII behind barbed wire.

Fitch was strafing a train over Europe when the Germans shot down his P-51 Mustang. He managed to convince his captors that the end of the war was near and good treatment of prisoners would result in it being easier on them when the Allies won. He ran a Corvette at Sebring in 1956, and also raced the SS in 1957. Shinoda was a child during the war but was rounded up with thousands of other Japanese-Americans who were interned in camps all over the U.S. After the war, he became a California hot-rodder and went to Michigan to join GM, becoming Bill Mitchell's "personal" designer in Mitchell's secret underground "Studio X."

77. The first AM/FM radios in the Corvette were offered in 1963.
Offered in mid-production, the vertically mounted radio had a sliding bar, but it lacked the signal-seeking feature of the "Wonderbar" radio it replaced.

78. Elvis Aaron Presley (one-time Tupelo, Mississippi, truck driver who later became the King of the crooners) was seen in the movie, "Clambake," driving the Stingray Special in the red livery it temporarily wore (at a time when it was also fitted with a 427 with four Webers visible through a clear bubble air scoop). In the movie, Elvis trades the Stingray for a motorcycle.
GM V.P. in charge of Design, William L. Mitchell, was a celebrity fan, inviting Kings, movie stars and astronauts to visit GM Design, where he always gave them the Royal tour. He wasn't alone in providing a dream car to the movie industry—Ford gave away the Lincoln Futura to a California customizer, George Barris, who turned it into the Batmobile.

79. The concept car called the Shark early in its career and Mako Shark I later in its career was built upon the XP-700 concept car, extinguishing the XP-700's career forever.
Even GM had some budget limits. Often show cars would go through iterations. Re-bodying a former show car also saves time when deadlines are approaching, such as an upcoming auto show. The principle reason for re-bodying the XP-700 was to be able to re-use the hand-made brass frame windshield and expensive double-bubble jet aircraft styled roof rather than transport those over to a new chassis.

80. GM's legal eagles have nightmares about GM prototypes being in private hands. Yet they lost several through the decades, like the XP-819 rear-engined Corvette, Cerv I single-seater, Cerv II four-wheel drive, and all SRs and Grand Sports.
The XP-819 slipped out when "Bunkie" Knudsen gave it to famed tuner Smokey Yunick who was supposed to cut it up for parts. A buyer saw the parts, bought it and resurrected it. The CERV I and CERV II were in the Briggs Cunningham Museum when

Cunningham abruptly sold his museum to a Florida man who sold off the two prototypes. The SR2 created especially for GM President Harlow Curtice was driven by him for only a short time until he grew bored with it and sold it to a lucky neighbor! Jerry Earl was not a GM employee, so when gifted by his father, he was free to sell his SR2. Somehow the Bill Mitchell SR2 also escaped. All five Grand Sports were leaked by Chevrolet Engineering to their racing friends lest they be ordered destroyed by an angry management who were bent on sticking to GM's pledge not to promote racing.

81. **The biggest help in reducing unsprung weight in the Sting Ray production car was independent rear suspension.**

The differential was frame mounted, moving it to the "sprung weight" category, which improved ride and handling. The suspension was a "three link" design with a trailing arm, lower lateral link or "strut rod," and a double u-jointed half-shaft delivering torque and acting as an upper lateral link.

82. **The Corvette was dominant in American SCCA racing in 1961 and 1962, but the Cobra came along in 1962 to threaten it, taking a firm hold in racing in 1964.**

The '63 Cobra weighed 1,000 lbs less than Chevy's production Corvette, plus Shelby had Ford backing on speed parts development, whereas GM waffled on speed parts development and blew hot and cold on supporting racing. Ford even designed the chassis of the big block 427 Cobra.

83. **The split rear window of the '63 Corvette was previewed nearly a decade in advance on the postwar GM show car, the Olds Golden Rocket.**

The boat-tail shape goes back to prewar Cord and Auburn Speedster. The Golden Rocket show car introduced in 1956 was influential enough for its roof to be briefly considered for the '56 Corvette. A full-size clay of the '56 Corvette featuring the roof was mocked up. But alas, the idea was tabled until the next generation process started.

84. **Hood louvers, knock-offs on the hubcaps, fender vents, and B-pillar air extraction vents were all features of the '63 Sting Ray production car that were simulated.**

For some reason, it was easier to simulate scoops and vents than make them functional, perhaps because making them functional would require additional finishing time. Gradually, as the years went on, there were less simulated and more functional styling features on the Sting Ray as the design was refined.

85. The convertible's body style was slightly more popular in the 1963 model year.

10,594 Coupes were sold. 10,919 convertibles were sold. The split-window sold surprisingly well considering it was a radical looking car. The coupe also cost a little over $200 more than the base one-top convertibles. Coupe production dwindled in their total percentage of production until the end of the body style with the '67 model.

86. *None* of the original Grand Sport Corvettes were built as roadsters.

All five were originally built as coupes. Duntov, a racing purist, believed race cars should have roofs because sometimes race cars turn over. Three were released as coupes, and two held back. Later, when those two were released, they had been converted by GM into roadsters. Dick Guldstrand, author of this book's introduction, raced a roadster version.

87. Although Harley Earl, GM's first VP in Charge of Styling (before the word "styling" was changed to the classier word "Design") retired in 1958, his friends at Design still built a custom '63 Sting Ray convertible for him and sent it to his retirement home in Palm Beach. The equipment used did not include a roof periscope because it was a convertible.

It was Earl's successor, William L. Mitchell, who was the champion of roof periscopes, using them on several Corvette show cars. Among the extra gauges on the "Earl Blue" Corvette was an altimeter, revealing Earl's love of aircraft gadgetry.

88. The Muncie gearbox, named after a town in Indiana, replaced the Borg-Warner 4-speed in late 1963. The first gear ratio in the wide-ratio Muncie that year was 2.56.

Actually GM had designed the Borg Warner T-10 and merely assigned outside vendor Borg-Warner to produce it. When they decided to manufacture the next generation themselves, they called it the "Muncie" but it was their design from the beginning. The previous T-10 wide-ratio in 1962 and 1963 had a 2.54 low.

89. The racing debut of the Z06 '63 coupe was at Riverside, at the Los Angeles Times Invitational Grand Prix on October 13, 1962. Mickey Thompson was not one of the lucky drivers piloting a new Z06 in this event.

Thompson, the famed drag racer and racing promoter, owned the car (numbered 119) that Hooper drove. Hooper won the race in the only '63 Sting Ray that finished. Thompson, at different times, had the ear of Chevy, Pontiac, and Ford and was often able to get cars and parts that officially didn't exist yet.

90. **Leather and air conditioning didn't become Corvette options until the introduction of the production Sting Ray in 1963.**
Air conditioning was introduced on the 'Vette in 1963. Three vents were provided, one in the console above the clock and an adjustable sphere at each of the far ends of the instrument panel. Leather was introduced, but only in one color choice—"Saddle Tan." Power windows had been previously available.

91. **The hotly sought-after Kelsey Hayes knock-offs first shown in 1963 were still available in 1966, and 1,194 brave souls actually ordered PRO P48 in 1966.**
The knock-offs required you hit them with a lead hammer to both remove or install them; many Corvette owners were not comfortable with this technique.

92. **The Corvette Shark show car originally had a 327 with Roots blower and dual sidedrafts for an engine.**
Mitchell used the car to drive to and from work and would switch the engine every few years. He favored aluminum ZL1 blocks and eventually had at least three Corvette prototypes fitted with that engine.

93. **The Corvette Grand Sport race car used Halibrand wheels, Girling brakes, and eventually Weber carburetion—parts not made by GM.**
GM hadn't gotten their lightweight wheel in production yet, nor did they have disc brakes and you couldn't beat the Italians for carburetion in the 1960s.

94. **When the first three Grand Sports were smuggled out to Chevy's racing friends, the 377 cu. in. V-8 did not go with them. They went out the door with production 360-hp F.I. engines.**
Duntov didn't have the engines ready when he first spirited three GS coupes out of the GM Tech Center. He had tested one in the original Stingray race car. But, by the Nassau Speed Weeks of late 1963, he was able to provide the 377-inchers, even though GM brass was watching him for violations of the AMA we-don't-race resolution. Somehow, since that event was run outside the U.S., it didn't matter to them.

95. **There was a 4-seater running prototype built of the 1963 Corvette because someone believed it would "expand the market." Ed Cole, General Manager at Chevrolet, was the champion of this 4-seater.**
Although the six-inch wheelbase stretch wasn't as objectionable visually as it sounds like it would be, Bill Mitchell hated it. Ed Cole saw it as a means of countering Ford's Thunderbird, which had

experienced a spurt in sales when it went 4-seater. The project lost all support when the then-President of GM, John Gordon, was invited to try out the seats in the rear of the prototype. He found that he needed help in order to extract himself. It's a good thing for 'Vette purists that Gordon was over six feet tall!

96. Zora Arkus-Duntov tested the independent rear suspension (I.R.S.) design for the '63 Corvette on the CERV I prototype.

Instead of building engineering test vehicles just for GM's test track, Zora tried to build a car that might relate to existing race classes. The mid-engined single-seater CERV I was built as a single-seater that was similar to a F1 car (Indy cars still being front-engined). It was used to test I.R.S. layouts. CERV I used coil springs in the rear while the '63 Corvette used a transverse leaf design. It later slipped out of GM's hands when they donated it to a museum and the museum owner dumped his entire collection to avoid tax liabilities.

97. In the case of a '63 Corvette, a rare option could you show your car with was 2-bar knock-offs; it looks wrong but is technically still correct.

When the '63 made its debut at the European shows, it sported two-bar knock-offs. However, when Corvettes arrived in the showroom, Chevrolet had already switched to three-barred knock-offs. Since they had shown the '63 at its world debut with two-bar knock-off spinners, conceivably one could still say that was correct, though, a really tough concourse judge might say their use was correct only if you could prove the car in question was one of the actual Paris or Geneva show cars built in the pilot line run. (Pilot line cars are cars built before full production starts to test assembly. They aren't supposed to be sold, but, as some are now appearing at Corvette events, it's obvious this wasn't strictly enforced.)

98. The problem with '63 Sting Rays ordered with cast aluminum Kelsey-Hayes knock-off wheels was the wheels were porous and leaked air.

Chevy shipped the cars with steel wheels and later offered the aluminum wheels at the parts counter. By 1964 the problem was solved.

99. The first year of the Sting Ray production car saw several race-theme colors on the color palette. Mulsanne Maroon was not a color in 1963.

During this era, GM Design named Corvette colors for racetracks. "Mulsanne" was not the name of a track but only a portion of a track—the long straight at LeMans in France. Corvette didn't use the name "Mulsanne" for a color until 1970, Mulsanne Blue. Bentley was a marque with indisputable rights to the name since they won LeMans outright more than once. They picked up "Mulsanne" as the name for a high performance model in the 1990s.

100. Independent rear suspension made the '63 coupe Corvette more comparable with the sophisticated sports cars of Europe.

Fuel injection dated back to 1957, disc brakes didn't come until 1965 and radial tires were not considered yet by American automakers. I.R.S. (independent rear suspension) represented the Corvette's Great Leap Forward for 1963.

101. Very early '63 Sting Rays had the letter "W" atop the new bolt-on top of the F. I. plenum chamber.

Supplier Winters Foundry thought the top surface was a nice place to put their snowflake logo and initial. Chevy thought otherwise and first created a blank space in place of the emblem and letter. Later they filled that blank space with a crossed flag emblem, used through 1965 models.

102. In 1964 a new addition to the interior was a bright chrome shift knob.

In 1963, the year before, the shift knob was black Bakelite. The teak wood wheel wasn't an available option until 1965.

103. On the 1964 model, rubber cushioned body-mounts and variable rate springs were added to enhance ride quality.

Gas-filled shock absorbers and air pumps for bladders in seats to inflate seat cushions came much later in the Corvette's career. The 1963 body was solidly bolted to the chassis, and the '63 springs were constant-rate. The '64 springs and body mount changes reduced noise, vibration, and harshness—what engineers called "NVH."

104. In 1964, one of the "simulated" styling features became real–the roof B-pillar vents. However, they were only functional on one side of the car.

The purpose was to vent the cockpit on the coupe of stale air. The simulated hood grates (copying the functional ones on the original Stingray race car) were dropped in 1964.

105. In 1964, 24 cars were shipped out in primer, without paint.

It was purposeful. The reason may have been a promotional one; perhaps some dealer was planning on painting them his own color so he could have a special model. Occasionally automakers will go along with a special request if the order is big enough. More than three decades later, they did a special paint job for an East Coast dealer's batch of Corvettes.

106. Of the 22,000 Corvettes made in 1964, a mere 806 had knock-off aluminum wheels.

Americans liked the looks but were probably still cautious about the sealing problems, which held back their availability soon after the 1963 introduction. Price may have been another deterring factor. P48 was an expensive option at $322.50.

107. Millions who attended the 1964 World's Fair saw a metallic candy apple red Corvette coupe at the GM display. The big block was not among the list of features of this one-off show car.

The big block wasn't offered until 1965 and maybe Chevy didn't want to tip their hand that it was coming. The editor recalls seeing this car cruising the drive-in restaurants along Woodward Avenue late one night, proving auto executives do get to play with the company toys on occasion. It was donated to the Blackhawk Museum in California in the 1990s.

108. The side-mount exhaust was introduced in 1965.

The RPO N14 side-mounts were continued through 1967 unchanged. An all-new design with a chrome-plated continuously-fluted cover was introduced on the Mako Shark-inspired body in 1969.

109. The 1965 Corvette had all of the following except the 390-hp big block option.

They had a big block option to be sure, the 396 cu. in. V-8, but it was rated at 425-hp. Antonick says 2,157 were built. And, even though that year had the great advance of disc brakes, if you were intent on resisting progress, you could still order drums!

110. Drag racers nicknamed the big block the "rat motor."

Of course, the small block was then inevitably called the "mouse motor."

111. 1965 marked the last year a Carter carburetor was offered in the Corvette.

The '65 327/250 and 327/300 were the last Corvette engines to sport Carters. In 1966 the 250-hp engine was dropped and the 300-hp with the Holley R-3367 carburetor became standard.

112. Shocking as it is, not all of the Corvette bodies from 1964-1967 were made by Chevrolet. In fact, about half of them came from A.O. Smith in Michigan, the same supplier who later built Shelby Mustangs from mid-1967 on.

These bodies were identified by an "A" (for A.O. Smith) rather than an "S" (for St. Louis) prefix on the body data plate found on the reinforcement under the glovebox. They arrived fully trimmed on triple deck railcars.

113. If you insisted, you could still get drum brakes on the '65. Chevy gave you back $64.50 in credit if you insisted on the drums.

The reasons for customers ordering them are unknown, but the fact was that Chevrolet had a pile of leftover drum brakes, so they were offered and there were orders.

114. 316 '65 Corvettes were ordered with drum brakes.

Discs were superior in both wet and dry weather but some Corvette buyers just weren't ready for this innovation.

115. Compared to the '65 Corvette, the '66 Corvette differed in badging because the '66 had the words "Corvette Sting Ray" on the hood.

The year 1966 was the only year of the Sting Ray era where the badge was on the hood itself.

116. An unusual feature of the 1966 and 1967 427s with Powerglide and A/C was an offset license plate bracket—to get more air into the grille cavity.

With the right (or wrong) options, Chevrolet feared the radiator wouldn't receive adequate airflow unless they moved the license plate out of the way.

117. M22 was the official designation for the gearbox known as the "rock crusher."

It was a very noisy but stronger gearbox due to the lower helix angle (20 deg. vs. 25 deg. on M20) gears, so you only ordered it if you were a serious racer. First official availability was 1966, but some experts document that at least 30 Corvettes went out the door so equipped in 1965.

118. Although it didn't include aluminum heads, the big block 396 offered in 1965 boasted features like the 4-bolt mains, impact extruded aluminum pistons, Holley 4-barrel carburetor, and the RPO K66 transistor ignition. The RPO K66 transistor ignition was a mandatory option with the big block.

Aluminum heads in the big block didn't come until 1967, in the L88 and L89.

119. In 1967, Dick Guldstrand and Bob Bondurant raced a Corvette L88 coupe at LeMans.

Sponsor was Dana Chevrolet. The car ran strong right into the 13th hour when they threw a rod and DNF'd. But, decades later, the car was rediscovered, restored and now is a popular sight at Corvette shows.

120. In 1965, when the big block made its debut, 51/49 was the weight distribution in the big block Corvette.

The chassis planners had done a good job so that even the heavier engine didn't throw the weight tremendously toward the front. The original small block was 48/52.

121. In 1965, fresh air fiends had their way and the majority of Corvettes ordered were convertibles. Out of 23,562 Corvettes made that year, 8,186 were coupes.

It was only a slight drop-off from the number of coupes sold the year before, when coupes were 37% of the total. In 1963, coupes were even higher, commanding 49% of Corvette sales.

122. The L88 introduced in 1967 had a Holley 4-barrel carburetor rated at 850 cfm.

The "double pumper" 850 had an accelerator pump at each end, and a center-pivot float so it wouldn't suffer from fuel starvation in the corners. According to Colvin, it was a type 4150 with mechanical secondaries with no provision for choke.

123. The "big block" for 1966 displaced 427 cu. in.

When asked at the 1966 press introduction why the displacement was increased, Duntov responded that boring the cylinders reduced weight. Everyone knew it was a tongue-in-cheek answer. The block required a new casting to accommodate the larger 4.25-inch bore.

124. The '66 coupe looked fairly similar to the '65, but vents that were on the roof pillars on the '65 were eliminated by 1966.

The '66 was originally intended to be the last of the Stingray race car-inspired body style, but it was carried over to 1967. It was cleaned up a little, with new horizontally-grooved rocker panel covers.

125. The L88s left off the choke, which would have been handy for street driving.

The Holley carburetor used had no choke on the L88 and ZL1. It was a racing engine, not meant for street driving.

126. GM gave a very specific recommendation in a paper label that was temporarily put on the console to tell you what fuel they preferred. They suggested an octane rating of 103.

On a paper tag attached with string set in the cockpit, GM gave specific recommendations on fuel, saying the fuel chosen should have a research octane number (RON) of at least 103 and a 95 motor octane number (MON). Sunoco 260 was one fuel that met those requirements.

127. Factory records show there were 20 L88 equipped Corvettes built in 1967.

Of course, you could buy L88 heads, pistons and camshaft at your Chevy dealer so many racers converted their big blocks to L88 specifications. However, the L88 package consisted of a lot more than that, such as J56 HD brakes, heater-delete and the fact that no radio could be ordered. If you tried to enter your Corvette in a concourse as an L88 just because you had L88 heads, air cleaner and hard scoop, it wouldn't fool anyone who knew the other parts that made a L88 legitimate.

128. In 1966, 15 customers went for the M22 rock crusher.

This was the first year for the M22 official availability, though some naturally assume it wasn't needed until 1967 when the L88 became available. Writer Alvin Colvin in *Chevrolet by the Numbers* says 32 were made in 1965 but no records show how many were fitted on Corvettes that year, though some were believed to have been installed. Corvette authority Antonick lists it as an option in 1965.

129. In 1967, the L71 435-hp option cost $437.00. If you wanted aluminum heads as well, the cost was an additional $368.65.

The L89 aluminum cylinder heads could only be ordered on top of the L71 435-hp option. A mere 16 sets were ordered.

130. Given the choice in 1967 between a big block and a small block, the small block engine was sold more.

Even with four big blocks from mild to wild listed on the order form, most customers still perceived the big block as a nose-heavy gas guzzler. So almost 70% of customers ordered small blocks, which came in 300-hp or 350-hp versions, the 300-hp version being the base engine.

131. Corvette buyers did not warm up to air conditioning very fast. Still, the percentage of buyers for the AC do show a steady rise from 1963—the first year of availability—on. However, the percentage never reached over 20 percent from 1963 through 1967.

The real answer is 17% or 3,788 out of 22,940 sold in 1967—the last year of the C2 body style. The public was still thinking of A/C as a performance-robbing addition and some didn't want to lose any of their precious horsepower on their Corvette.

132. The "tanker" wasn't so desirable by 1967. Only two people ordered it.

Why? Because the C2 body style was getting a little old by 1967, and racers who wanted to race Corvettes were already looking at the all-new '68.

133. If you ordered your Corvette with RPO C48 in 1967, that referred to the heater-defroster delete.

Option C48 was mandatory that year with the L88. This was Zora Arkus-Duntov's idea to make sure that uninformed buyers wouldn't buy a very hot racing Corvette and try to street drive it. The theory? Race cars don't need heaters. Make them uncomfortable and only the purists will order it. In all, 35 people opted for that option, all receiving a credit of $97.95. Not all 35 cars were L88s.

134. In 1967, the factory was forced to install big block hoods on a few small block equipped cars.

When some klutz dropped something on the tooling for the small block hood, damaging it, they quickly ran out of small block hoods. Rather than hold the cars in storage without hoods, big block hoods went out on some '67s but without the wide stripe on the hood hump and painted "stinger."

135. In 1967 models, the air scoop with the L88 engine option pulled in the most air.

This ought to be a slam-dunk as it was the only one of all the big block hoods that came with functional air inlets (at the aft, or windscreen, end). All the other scoops were non-functional.

136. Many racetrack-derived color names offered on the '67 Corvettes are from U.S. racetracks or U.S. towns where tracks were located, like Elkhart Blue, Lynndale Blue, and Marlboro Maroon.

Goodwood is a track to be sure but it's a track in England. Elkhart Lake is in Wisconsin, the town where the Road America track is located. Lynndale is in Illinois, Marlboro in Maryland.

137. For 1967, the aluminum wheels from the factory were distinguished by no knock-off spinner, but five lug nuts.

However, the lug nuts were covered by a tasteful cover, which provided a "cross-laced" effect, its outer rim "spokes" intermeshing with the spokes of the center portion.

138. Compared with the L88's single quad and the ZL1's single quad, the three two-barrels on the '67 carburetor system the had the highest rated airflow.

The "trips" had a combined airflow rating of over 1,276 cfm and the Holley 4-barrel was rated at 850 cfm. However, carburetor airflow varies as the square root of pressure drops. Two-barrel carburetors are measured at a 3.0-inch Hg depression, four barrels at 1.5-inch Hg. Two barrels can be converted to four-barrel airflow by multiplying the two-barrel flow by 0.71. Then you come out with a bit over 906 cfm, slightly more than the L88 and ZL1's 850 cfm four barrel. Besides that, the "trips" were hard to tune. Offering them was basically a marketing gimmick.

139. For 1967, five gills for the side vent, a rear back-up light above the license plate, and a new hood scoop design for the big block were all new features.

The '67 was a "continuation model" with a few updates. The T-top, with two roof hatches fastening to a center bar, didn't come to the Corvette until the 1968 Mako-Shark-inspired model.

140. The standard side vent window and optional side pipes available on the '67 Corvette disappeared when they brought out the '68.

"Astro-ventilation" was supposed to make up for the lack of vent windows. It didn't. Side-mount exhausts became available again in 1969 but were a completely different design.

141. In the '67, they relocated the parking brake between the bucket seats.

By getting rid of the "knee knocker" under the instrument panel, they made the car more European. The new location made the brake easier to work if you were on a hill.

142. In 1967, the U15 speed warning was an option introduced on the Corvette for the first time.

Periodically government agencies were making noise about limiting the speed of vehicles. Chevrolet offered this warning device to show that they were sensitive to safety issues. Back in early 1963, the speed warning had been tied to engine speed, not mph like the 1967 unit. A total of 2,108 were sold at $10.55 each.

143. The '67 was an "emergency" carry-over from 1966 because the car that became the '68 wasn't ready for introduction as a '67. Nonetheless, the '67 got a few updates so buyers wouldn't feel they were buying an "old" design. A white vinyl top for the hardtop was not offered as an option.

There was a vinyl top covering option offered for the hardtop but, like Henry's Model T Ford, the only color available was black. If you didn't order RPO C08 with your hardtop, it came painted the same color as the car.

144. An aluminum block was not part of the L88 package introduced in 1967.

Heads, yes, but not the block. That privilege went to the optional ZL1 big blocks introduced, albeit ever so momentarily, in 1969. It wasn't until the 1997 C5-series that an aluminum block became standard in all Corvettes.

The Mako Shark Era

145. In 1968, when it came to big block heads, you could tell at a glance (when the engine is apart) if they were medium or high horsepower by the shape of the inlet ports.

The 390 and 400 had oval inlet ports; the higher-powered 435 had rectangular ports. The other answers don't deal with heads.

146. Bob Wingate was not a National Champion in a Corvette.

Wingate was a famous West Coast Corvette salesman, first at Clippinger Chevrolet in Covina, California, and then with his own business.

147. Engine codes L0, LV, and MR indicated ultra-rare L88 engines in 1969.

The non-L88 numbers shown were LP designatng L89 heads on L71 with manual transmission and LX designating the L71 435-hp big block with automatic transmission.

148. The aluminum block ZL1 was first available in the Corvette in 1969.

The all-aluminum big block was a spin-off of the program to develop engines for Can-Am racing cars like the McLaren and Chaparral. Chevy offered it very briefly in Corvettes, but Chevy dealers were able to order a total of 69 Camaros with the ZL1 in order to counter Ford's Cobra-Jet Mustang in drag racing.

149. Only two ZL1 Corvettes are thought to have been built in 1969.

Contrast this with the fact the Camaro, a sporty car somewhat lower on the sporty car totem pole, got dozens of ZL1 engines compared to Corvette's scant two. This short-changing of GM's flagship is inexplicable when the Corvette was supposed to be GM's flagship sports model, but there you are...

150. Winters Foundry, in Canton, Ohio cast the ZL1 blocks.

Right—the same folks who did the Ram Jet fuel injection units back in the early 1960s. Although the casting was first done at Winters, the machining and assembly was done at Tonawanda, New York.

151. The L88 was the Godzilla option for 1968, the year that 80 were sold.

More were sold than in 1967 as word began to spread about how much power the engine really produced (something close to 550 hp). Price of the engine was $947.20.

152. There were two series of L88 engines. The second series had changes to go along with the new open chamber cylinder heads that were better for emissions, and to allow more compatibility with lower octane fuel.

The new design came on stream approximately April 1969.

153. 17 L88s were automatics in 1969.

While the transmission was labeled TurboHydramatic 400 and had the same ratios (2.48, 1.48 and 1.00) as the other TBH400s, it had internal changes to the clutches and modulator in order to cope with the powerful engine. Plus you had to pay $290.40 for it vs. $221.80 for the other engines.

154. The L88 got a heater in 1968 and 1969, which it lacked in 1967.

GM had originally required the C48 heater-deletion option in the L88 to discourage anyone from ordering it as a street driver. They relented because new Federal Motor Vehicle Safety Standards (FMVSS) required windshield defrosters, and in order to have a defroster you have to have a heater.

155. The '67 L88 had a proportioning valve and dual-pin front brake calipers as part of its braking system that other Corvettes that year didn't.

The Special Heavy-duty Brakes proportioning valve was to limit rear brake line pressure. The dual pins held things together better.

156. Back in 1969, ZL1 engine codes stamped into the blocks were either ME or MG.

Both were for 427/430 alloy block engines with the ME designating a block ordered with a M22 manual 4-speed and the MG for a 3-speed automatic. Although an automatic-equipped "mule" (engineering prototype) was flogged by reporters at the preview for the 1969 models, that doesn't automatically mean one was ever sold. Still, there's many a slip twixt the cup and the lip and sometimes individuals are able to buy what was originally intended for test only.

157. James Garner, star of the "Maverick" TV series, decided to get into racing just as the Corvette switched from the Stingray-inspired body to the Mako-shark-inspired body. He ordered two L88 '68 Corvettes, formed a team called American International Racers, and fielded them in the 24 Hours of Daytona in February, 1968.

Drivers were Dick Guldstrand, Ed Leslie and Herb Caplan (in car #44) and Scooter Patrick and Dave Jordan (in car #45). They were able to start in the front row, having trounced all the others in practice, but only one of the two finished—#44 at 29th overall. After that the team switched to Lola T-70s. Eastwood never had a race team; Newman sponsored Lolas, Nissans and Ferraris; Blocker was an early Can-Am sponsor.

158. Triple carburetion was not a feature of the almighty 1969 ZL1.

The 4-barrel Holley provided better mixture distribution so "trips" weren't necessary. Even when triple carburetors were available on the other big blocks, they were more marketing gimmickry than necessity.

159. By the end of 1969, 216 L88s had rolled out the doors of the St. Louis factory since the engine package was first offered in 1967.

It wasn't many but there weren't that many real racers, and that's who Chevrolet had developed the engine for.

160. In a move reminiscent of the early days of the '53 Corvette (when the Corvettes were sold to VIPs and various and sundry high mucky-mucks), in 1969, three specially modified Corvette coupes were delivered to three Apollo 12 astronauts.

The trio was Pete Contrad, Dick Gordon, and Al Bean. The cars were all-matching Riverside Gold 390-hp 427s, automatics, with PO2 deluxe wheel covers, and black rear deck paint. They also had three-color decals (red, white and blue) on the fenders containing the astronaut's rank such as CMR. (Oh, and don't tell us about the Corvettes used in the movies about astronauts. Hollywood always gets the Corvettes wrong.)

161. Although the 1968 Corvette was inspired by the Mako Shark II show cars (there were two of them, a non-runner and a runner) the '68 adopted the body shape but left out many details.

The Inside Scoop

Although the production '68 came out with that style of "tunnel back" or "sugar scoop" roof with an upright rear window flanked by sail panels, the Mako Shark II in its first incarnation had a teardrop fastback with louvers that would go flat at the touch of a button. The Mako Shark II finally got a sugar scoop rear roof in its makeover into the "Manta Ray" late in its career. Side exhausts from the Manta Ray inspired those on the '69-and-later production Corvettes.

162. Tony DeLorenzo and Jerry Earl happened to have fathers who were high GM brass (and who helped them obtain special Corvette race cars).

DeLorenzo's father was head of GM Public Relations, while Earl's father was Harley Earl, GM's first director of Design (called the Art and Colour section before WWII). He ordered the first SR2 built in order to discourage his son from racing a Ferrari. The younger Earl's car was a "gift" from the Old Man. GM brass later forbid such gift cars. DeLorenzo paid for his cars; later he sold them (there were several team cars). The Earl SR2 and at least one of the Owens-Corning team cars have been restored and are sometimes seen at Corvette conventions.

163. On the changeover from 1967 to 1968, side-mount exhausts were dropped, only to reappear in 1969.

The '68 Corvette designers were proud of the "coke bottle" shape and thought side pipes might detract from the purity of the shape. Consumer demand forced sidepipes back on the 'Vette in 1969, but with a different design than the '67 Corvettes.

164. In the 1969 Corvette, the outside door release differed from the 1968 model.

For 1969, the separate button from 1968 was gone. It was replaced by a one-purpose outside door lock-handle combination.

165. The year 1969 saw a huge fall-off in convertible acceptance in the Corvette.

In 1968 coupes were 34.8% of the total Corvettes but the next year (1969) saw coupes jump to 57.2%, indicating customer displeasure with the ragtop version of the "Mako-inspired" 'Vette. Convertibles were discontinued in 1976 on the mistaken assumption T-tops would satisfy fresh air fiends. Eleven years later, in 1986, they came back by popular demand in the C4.

166. Engines L46 and LT1 offered in 1970 were not available with an automatic transmission.

Both performance small blocks, they lacked sufficient low end torque and idle quality for Chevy to offer an automatic. The L46 was the hydraulic lifter 350 /350 with a Quadrajet and the LT1 the mechanical lifter 350 /370 with a Holley.

167. **According to expert Karl Ludvigsen, the '68 Corvette achieved a 0.84 lateral g-force reading on the skidpad.**
This was a highly respectable reading. Only mid-engined cars could do better at the time.

168. **The Corvette XP-819 engineering research car, De Tomaso Vallelunga, Matra D'Jet, De Tomaso Mangusta, and Corvette XP-880 engineering research car, all 2-seaters, had a backbone-type chassis.**
The center beam was tried on several experimental Corvettes. The 819 had a Y-like split aft of the rear wheels, that "Y" carrying the engine so it was actually rear-engined. The XP-880, also called the Astro II during its show career, had an almost identical frame but its engine was placed amidships.

169. **Because of a long strike one year, GM thought it necessary to extend the model year into the next year's time. The model year that was extended was 1969, until December of that year.**
There were 38,762 sold that year compared to over 10,000 less the year before. The '84 model year also enjoyed a longer than usual production period; they started early because they had cancelled the '83 model year outright for the Corvette. In 1983, it wasn't "better-late-than-never," just "never."

170. **In the movie *Con Air*, starring Nicholas Cage, a pristine blue Sting Ray roadster is snagged by a transport plane trailing a sky hook, yanked into the wild blue, then dropped like a hot rock. It was a '67 model, reportedly the same year that the actor owns in his stable of sports cars.**
Don't worry, they didn't wreck a *real* '67—you can do a lot with smoke and mirrors.

171. **For 1968, a lot of colorful cows were needed to provide the leather, but alas, that year no interiors came in white.**
For some reason, white has been a very rare option in Corvette history, despite that there is a small niche of car buyers who will buy a model with white paint, white interior and white top.

172. **Zora Arkus-Duntov's CERV II could have gone up against the Ford GT40s at LeMans.**
But, alas, it remained a research and development vehicle. Duntov in a way paved the way for Porsche to bring out a 4WD production car decades later. The CERV II was secretly tested against Jim Hall's Chaparrals several times, and it was no accident that parts from

GM's mid-engined experimental cars sometimes migrated over to Hall's Chaparrals, which did, in fact, occasionally act as a "spoiler" to blunt Ford's racing efforts with the Ford GTs in Europe.

173. The cylinder heads of the late 1969 L88s and ZL1s were known as open chamber heads.

The closed chamber heads were offered in the L88 from 1967 to 1969 to approximately SN 22,000. After that it was open chamber heads. The change was made for emissions but they improved performance as well.

174. A.I.R. had to be added to the L88 in 1968 and 1969 in order to meet emissions.

No, it didn't stand for "American International Racing" (James Garner's Team which ran Corvettes) but for "Air Injection Reactor." Your '68 or '69 L88, or ZL1 is not "correct" without it.

175. The ZL1 block was finished in *au natural* aluminum (just in case you find one on a used car lot).

Why paint it when you have such a unique selling proposition in an aluminum block? It had iron cylinder liner sleeves and 4-bolt main caps.

176. The ZL1 option package cost $4,718.35 in 1969.

A crazy price for an option package considering that the base price of the coupe was $4,781. Many sources simplify and say $3,000, but that figure doesn't include all the mandatory options you had to order with a ZL1, which pushed the price up.

177. The LT1 was first available in 1970.

The 350 cu. in. engine size came the year before but the 370-hp LT1 version didn't come until 1970. It was the first year for solid lifters since 1965.

178. The LT1 was the hot small block with a solid lifter cam, Holley carburetor and high revs, but at first air conditioning wasn't available with it.

It was thought the engine wound so high it was all too easy to throw belts (as this author did in his 350.) Eventually Duntov pulled one off the line, had it fitted with A/C, determined it functioned normally and it was then made available with air conditioning late in the 1972 model year.

179. 1,287 LT1 packages were sold in 1970 for $447.60 each.

The LT1 was thought of as a small block with big block power.

180. When you ordered the ZR1 package with the LT1, you got J56 HD brakes.

The brakes were racing units featuring dual-pin front calipers, special front brake pad backing plates, special brake pad compounds, etc. In previous year, the J56 HD brakes were listed as a separate option.

181. The ZR1 package was first offered in 1970.

The ZR1 package was, basically, a racer package built around the small block consisting of HD suspension, heavy-duty power brakes, special rear wheel spindle strut shafts, M22 4-speed, transistor ignition, aluminum radiator, HD shocks, and a metal fan shroud. Off-putting was the fact that many options weren't orderable with it as well. Most experts agree 25 were produced that year, the optional package costing $968.95.

182. Chevrolet adopted "Monaco Orange" in 1969 as a color name.

Monaco has always been a Formula One site, laid out once a year in the city streets of the Principality of Monaco. The original Carrera Panamericana races ended just as the Corvettes were first being produced. Porsche's victories there entitled them to use the "Carrera." Tripoli was a pre-war event. Chevy felt entitled to use "LeMans" for a color name as Corvettes had competed at the Sarthe circuit as far back as 1960 when Briggs Cunningham fielded his 3-car effort.

183. Side-mount exhausts were a popular option in 1969. 4,355 customers ordered them.

That was a lot of sidepipes (at $147.45 a set) considering the fact that, in some municipalities, cops were still writing tickets for "excessive noise" from something that, by virtue of being a listed option should have been considered to be "original equipment."

184. Only the mechanical-lifter engines required K66 Transistor Ignition as a mandatory option in 1969.

You could order it as an option on the L68, a hydraulic lifter big block, but it was not mandatory on the small block L46 or L68. Chevrolet says 5,702 K66 Transistor Ignitions were sold in 1969 at $81.00 each.

185. In April 1970 Chevrolet showed the XP-882, a mid-engined Corvette, at the New York Auto Show. However, they weren't the only Detroit automakers showing a mid-engined sports car powered by a made-in-U.S.A. V-8. The AMX/III and the DeTomaso Pantera were also shown.

Ford introduced the DeTomaso Pantera in 1971, importing it through 1974. American Motors (AMC) only made six AMX/IIIs as prototypes. Although the Monteverdi Hai used an American-made Chrysler 426 Hemi engine, it wasn't sponsored by any

The Inside Scoop

American automaker and the two or three that came to the U.S. were brought in as "gray market" imports by individuals.

186. The 1970 LT1 had a decal between pin stripes on each side of the power dome reading "LT1" on the hood to identify it.

For some reason, although it was a popular engine, it didn't rate its own chrome letter badge like the 427 did. But at least it got the big block's power dome hood.

187. For the 1970 model year, the LS6 and LS7 were both praised mightily in the press but failed to materialize in a Corvette that year.

The LS6 was essentially a '66 L72 enlarged to 454 cu. in. It did show up in the Chevelle in 1970 but not the Corvette. The LS7 was no-show as well.

188. For the 1970 model year, the LS7 was again praised mightily but failed to materialize in any year Corvette.

The LS7 was a racing engine like the L88, producing something over 550 hp. This gorilla was too fierce to let out of its cage so it was offered only over the counter as a "crate engine." The confusion over availability started when some magazines, including *Sports Car Graphic*, ran driving impressions based on a prototype loaned to them by Chevrolet. But Chevy got cold feet and cancelled it from the production slate.

189. You have probably figured by now that the LS6 engine was offered in the Corvette eventually. In 1971, this monster mill was rated at 425 hp.

After all the hype, a mere 188 were sold.

190. In 1970 when you ordered the ZR1 package, Chevrolet forbid you from ordering air conditioning, a rear window defroster, wheel covers, a radio, power steering, automatic transmission, power windows, and an alarm system.

In short, if you ordered this serious package, you better be the type who likes to go long on racing bits and short on creature comforts. Only 25 were built.

191. In 1971, the ZR1 option, called the Special Performance Engine Package, was still offered. Slalomers were thought to be champing at the bit to order it, but only eight were sold.

In truth, although a lot of people talked about ordering a heavy-duty package, they really wanted creature comforts and when they saw the long list of options they wouldn't be able to order with the ZR1, most of them lost their desire for the package. The package price, at $1,010, may have been off-putting as well.

192. In 1970, John Greenwood was GT class winner at Sebring, along with Dick Smothers as co-driver.

Smothers also shared a Corvette at LeMans in 1972, lasting only 10 laps before losing a piston. He was a serious racer, and car collector, and later went into the winery business.

193. The Corvette Mulsanne concept car, based on a production coupe, had the following unusual features: non-flip up headlamps, roof periscope, ZL1 engine, side-mount exhausts, cross-laced wheels, and "ghost" flames.

The Mulsanne was a Mitchell's styling hack that he had re-done every time he wanted to see how a new trend would look. It was candy apple red, silver, and metalflake ice blue at different times and even sported pinstriped "shadow" or "ghost" (outlined) flames. Like the Shark, it had a roof periscope. Several engines were tried. A one-piece roof was installed so that, during pace car duties at Can-Am races, the passenger serving as flagman could better monitor the line-up or race cars behind them.

194. In 1973 there was a leather seat color called "Dark Saddle."

In the years before there was "Saddle Tan" as introduced in 1963, but in 1973 there was both "Medium Saddle" and "Dark Saddle."

195. The 1969 Corvette had map pockets added to give it more of a European flavor.

A feature of European cars for decades, the map pockets were to the right of the console.

196. 1970 was the first year of the 454.

Derived from the 427, the bore was the same at 4.25 inches, but the stroke went from 3.76 inches to 4.0 inches.

197. 9:1 was the compression ratio of the monster mill LS6 offered in 1971.

You thought it would be higher, right? Ah, if you did, you forgot The General's promise to make all 1971 engines operate on unleaded fuel. It probably cost enthusiasts 40-50 lbs-ft. of torque across the rev range compared to what it would have had with an 11.0:1 compression ratio.

198. In 1971 you could order an automatic with the powerful LS6 but not if you ordered the ZR2 package.

In 1971, the automatic transmission was not permitted to be sold with the ZR1 or ZR2 packages because both of these packages were developed for road racers. However, you could order an LS6 in a non-ZR2 packaged Corvette and still have a very potent engine mated to an automatic, making an excellent drag racer.

199. In 1971, 12 big blocks were sold with their "racer" package—the ZR2.

Since emissions controls were coming on strong, the mechanical lifter alloy-headed 425-hp 454 cu. in. LS6 was the last gasp of Corvette performance for quite a while to come. The ZR2 package included LS6, M22, F41, HD suspension, HD brakes, and V01 aluminum heavy-duty radiator—in short everything the L88 had except the efficient cowl induction hood scoop.

200. 1972 was the last year for the pop-out rear window in the Mako Shark-inspired production Corvette.

The removable back window option was dropped after the '72 model year. An unexpected bonus was more luggage space once the rear window was permanently fixed in place, this because there had been a rack in the back area to hold the window once it was removed.

201. The Corvette Four-Rotor had two engines at the time of its premiere.

While they were already building the Two-Rotor show car, GM wanted to show how big they were on the rotary engine, by also making a really spectacular mid-engine car with a bigger engine. Mercedes and Mazda had four-rotor mid-engined prototypes but there was no time for GM to engineer one so 2 Two-Rotor GMREs were lashed together with chain drive and a 390 cu. in. displacement figure quoted to make it sound like there was only one engine. It fooled almost everybody at the time.

202. "Route 66" was the title of a CBS TV series that originally ran between 1960 and 1964, starting a new Corvette piloted by Martin Milner as "Tod" and George Maharis as "Buz."

The premise was a bit thin, a son inherits a '61 'Vette and, with a buddy, heads out for the open road, in this case Route 66, a stretch of blacktop that ran from Chicago to Santa Monica, California. The series showed their interaction (i.e. meddling) with the folks they met along the way. As the years went on, the 'Vette they used kept getting updated with no explanation (he kept re-inheriting new ones?). There was an attempt to revive the series with four new pilots shot in 1993, but the magic imbued by the original Route 66—where you actually met real people in real towns—was gone and the pilots didn't get picked up as a series.

203. The rarest drivetrain feature you probably have ever heard of on a Corvette is a dual-disc clutch. It was standard equipment on the LS6.

The press had discussed the availability of a dual-disc clutch as an option as early as 1969, but it was a no-show. After first appearing on a prototype LS7 shown to reporters at a long-lead preview in 1970, it finally appeared as standard equipment on the LS6 in 1971.

204. Because they had success with the '82 Collector's Edition on the outgoing C3 body style, Chevrolet marketers decided for a little dèjà vu, doing the same thing in 1996.

But you would have to say the '96 wasn't as elaborate. It came in Sebring silver metallic with matching ZR1-style wheels; 17-inch tall wearing P255/45ZR17 tires in front and P285/40ZR17 rears. The brake calipers were painted black with silver lettering that read, "CORVETTE." The LT1 was standard, the LT4 optional. Maybe Chevy hoped to sell a bunch to C4 traditionalists who didn't like the "Spy" pictures of the upcoming C5. They sold 5,412 of them.

205. The XP-895 mid-engined Corvette show car was built by automotive industry supplier, Reynolds Aluminum.

The aluminum supplier was anxious to prove to Chevrolet that the Corvette could be bodied in aluminum at a reasonable cost, so they bankrolled the building of an alternative notchback design on a spare XP-882 chassis. The alloy-bodied car saved 40% in weight over a steel car but the cost still came out at three times higher than the cost of steel. An engineer working on the CERV IV mid-engined Corvette experimental car found the XP-895 in storage decades later and talked Chevrolet into letting him have a budget to restore it. It now makes occasional appearances.

206. One of the rarest decals you'll ever find atop the air cleaner on a 1966 big block is "450-hp."

It was an insurance issue. The Corporation periodically panicked that insurance companies would charge overly high premiums if they published horsepower figures that were too high, so after first releasing the horsepower figure of "450-hp" as a Corvette decal in 1966 they later switched to a 425-hp rating decal, which seemed tamer, if only by a little. In 1970 they had no such compunction when offering the LS6 in the Chevelle where it proudly wore a 450-hp decal. Over 4,000 LS6 Chevelles were sold.

207. Magnesium calipers were not a feature of the ZR1 and ZR2 package's brakes in the early 1970s.

Use of lightweight calipers in regular road cars hadn't come into use in American cars yet.

208. The difference between "gross" and "net" ratings that caused the big "drop" in Corvette power ratings in 1972 was as follows: Gross was engine out of the car with unrestricted exhaust and all power accessories off. Net was with engine as installed in car, with production exhausts, accessories and fan installed and all power robbing accessories in place.

The listed power output dropped about 20%, say from 425-hp to 350-hp, but the net ratings were more representative of the real world. GM liked it because it reduced government criticism but to enthusiasts it seemed that—without the big numbers of the past to quote—a lot of power had been "stolen." "Net" was also corrected to a lower density.

209. The LS6 was a bargain at $1,221.00.

It included aluminum heads instead of the iron heads as on the Chevelle version, a mechanical lifter cam and a Holley four-barrel; lots of premium parts.

210. The first year of the soft front bumper on the Corvette nose was 1973.

The energy absorbing material and draw bolts were hidden under a urethane cover. Unfortunately these covers faded at a different rate than the paint on the body. The chrome back bumper was still there in 1973.

211. In 1971, there were two "Z" special performance packages mated to high performance engines.

If you ordered the ZR2 suspension package, it required the big block LS6. This was for slalomists/autocrossers who believed big block torque is what won. If you ordered the ZR1 suspension package, you had to order the LT1 high winding small block. This was built for road racers.

212. In 1976, Chevrolet reintroduced the same style of slotted "mag" wheel they had previously introduced but then recalled in 1973.

The American company Kelsey-Hayes was the supplier, and cast the wheels in their Mexican foundry. RPO Y78 was a $299 option. This time 6,253 sets were sold.

213. You would think the last year of the big block (1974) would have resulted in a great rush of orders from big block believers. However, the actual percentage of big blocks ordered was 10 percent.

The big block had 20 more horsepower than the L82 but, ironically, the big block LS4 was cheaper to build and cost the customer less than the L82 (which had a lot of premium parts). The LS4 was $250, the L82 was $299. The 1973 energy crisis—with people all over America waiting in long lines for fuel—might have been a factor contributing to the slump in big block demand as well.

214. A rare Special Performance Equipment package ordered in 1973 was Z07.

It could only be ordered with the L82 or LS4 engine and required the M21 4-speed manual close-ratio transmission. It was more than just a suspension package. It included the HD brakes, high rate front and rear springs, larger diameter front and rear anti-roll bars, and specific shocks. It started out in 1973 at roughly $369, then went to $400 in 1974 and 1975. Only 45 Z07s were sold in the 1973 model year.

215. FE7 was a bargain-basement priced suspension package offered in 1974.

FE7 was the designation for the Gymkhana suspension. It included a stiffer front sway bar and stiffer springs. It could be ordered on any Corvette regardless of engine or transmission. In 1974 there were 1,905 Corvettes sold with FE7. And no wonder—the "package" costs only seven bucks!

216. When GM stopped experimenting with the rotary engine in the mid-1970s, the sleek silver gullwinged Four-Rotor Corvette was saved from the scrap heap by having its name magically transformed overnight to "Aerovette."

Bill Mitchell loved the word "aero" (maybe because he wrote aircraft instrumentation instruction guides while serving in the Navy during the war). Like many at Design, he couldn't bear to see the gullwinged Four-Rotor tossed into the dustbin along with GM's rotary engine. With its new name it also got a good ol' low-tech 400 cu. in. pushrod V-8. The car can be seen today at Corvette events.

217. The L82 of 1978 gave you 220 horsepower.

A dual snorkel air intake, a hot hydraulic cam and other premium parts were all ingredients of the $525 package that gave you 25 more horses than the base L48.

218. The catalytic converter became standard on the Corvette in 1975.

Dual exhausts were still on the Corvette, but what you couldn't see from the back of the car was that the duals ran from the engine to a single converter, then split again to exit out the back of the car. This spelled the end to any return of side-mounts because there was no consideration given to having two expensive catalytic converters.

219. **In 1975 High Energy Ignition was added to complement the catalytic converter.**

A highly reliable ignition system was needed with the catalytic converter because a misfiring engine could quickly overheat the catalytic converter.

220. **The alphanumeric code for the Silver Anniversary Corvette was RPO B2Z.**

15,283 were sold. Among the options you got with it were sport mirrors and aluminum wheels.

221. **Deep tinted glass roof panels were first offered in 1977, and then retracted from availability in a squabble between Chevrolet and its supplier over sales rights.**

The option returned in 1978, from another supplier. Lesson learned: if you want to be a supplier, you don't mess with The General. The vendor managed to sell his supply on the aftermarket under the name "Moonroof."

222. **When Chevrolet had to hasten to meet the 5-mph bumper laws, for the '74 model they devised a soft plastic cover for the back of the Corvette to cover the energy absorber. What characterized the '75 version of this end cap was that it was a one-piece.**

The earlier two-piece was looked down upon as too obvious. Another problem with the Endura end cap was that it changed color at a different rate than the Corvette body. When you painted it, you had to have a paint with a "flex agent" so the paint didn't crack.

223. **In 1975, few noticed the Z07 package was still on the option list. The suspension and brake package included twin-pin heavy-duty brake calipers, stiffer springs front and rear, a larger front anti-roll bar, a rear anti-roll bar and required the M21 4-speed manual. There were 144 ordered that year. By 1975, if you wanted performance, new emissions and safety laws had taken so much out of the new Corvette that if you wanted to race one, you had to buy an older one.**

The rarity of some options can only be explained by the fact that those who order new Corvettes don't read the option lists as diligently as the hobbyists of 30 years later, who roundly curse the first owners for not buying this or that option that would have immeasurably increased the value of the Corvette they ordered for future collectors in decades hence.

224. **On March 15, 1977 another production milestone was reached in St. Louis—500,000 Corvettes built.**

Even with dips in the economy and a body style that originated almost a decade earlier, they were selling well. A white coupe with red interior was the car that won this honor.

225. The Corvette Silver Anniversary came along in 1978.

Similar to Jim Beam whiskey distillers, GM accidentally discovered that event-linked limited editions sold like hot cakes, especially to collectors who salt the commemorative piece away in hopes of reaping profits later.

226. The year 1970 was Corvette's first for rectangular exhaust tips.

Considering the body style had been the same since 1968, the rectangles gave the Corvette's aft view a fresh look. The rectangular tips were offered through the '73 model year.

227. Chevrolet originally announced they were going to build 2,500 1978 Indy Pace Car replicas.

The original idea had been to build 100 to mark each year of Corvette production. Soon after announcement, they began to catch heat from Chevrolet dealers, some of whom were worried they wouldn't get one. So they increased the production run to 6,502, so there would be one for every dealer plus a couple of hundred extras for any dealer who might complain that they needed more than one.

228. The '78 Pace Car Replicas came with most of their special equipment installed except for the decals, which were left to the owner to install.

At $13,653.21, the Pace Car Package was priced roughly $4,000 above a base coupe. Providing the decals separately was a wise move, because not everybody wanted to go around pretending they were Boy Racer with all the decals, but they liked the package's other unique features.

229. If you have a two-tone '81 Corvette with its original paint job, your car was built in Bowling Green, Kentucky.

The paint facility at the new plant in Bowling Green was state of the art and they could cope with two-tone easier than the St. Louis plant, which was winding down its operations that year.

230. In 1982, 6,759 Collector Editions were sold.

With enough "sneak peeks" at the next generation Corvette having been leaked in the press, there might have been some who preferred the "Mako Shark" body style and decided to order one last one of that style, and to order it in this well-packaged special edition. It cost $22,537.59, or roughly $4,200 more than the standard coupe.

231. The year 1981 saw Corvettes being produced simultaneously at two different GM plants in two different states.

GM didn't want to lose availability of product during the switchover from the old plant in St. Louis, Missouri, to the new plant in Bowling Green, Kentucky, so they continued building 'Vettes in St. Louis, while workers relocated individually to Kentucky. When they had a full staff in Kentucky, they began building cars and when they got the line up to full speed, they closed down the St. Louis plant. The last Corvette rolled out of the St. Louis plant's door August 1, 1981. It was just as well—it was kind of embarrassing to admit the Corvette was being built in a plant that went back to the days of horse-drawn wagons.

232. In 1982, a new engine designation was on the flanks of the Corvette. The name "Cross Fire" refers to dual throttle body injection (TBI).

Fuel injection was installed the first time around on Corvettes solely for performance but this time around it was for emissions, as TBI produced more precise fuel metering than a carburetor. The manifold was a cross-ram type unit in which the long intake runners feed cylinders on the opposite bank, creating a ram effect.

233. The '78 Pace Car had quite a "few" options included in the package. NA6, which would have been an option on other Corvettes that year, was not included in the Pace Car's base price.

NA6 was the high altitude package. It wouldn't be needed by most buyers, unless they lived in Denver or other towns above 5,000 feet. The Pace Car package was capitalizing on the fact that Chevrolet had discovered those ordering Limited Editions wanted them for showing off and grand touring so they would have loaded them anyway. The package cost roughly $4,300 more than the base model.

234. The first official "Collector Edition" came in 1982. It was available in only one color, and that was silver-beige, paint code 59.

GM already knew that there would be a few who would miss the "Shark-based" Corvette so they thought they would make a special model in the last year of that body style. It had 200-hp, a lift-up rear hatch, a power antenna, deep-pile carpeting, "turbine" alloy wheels, white-letter P255/60 Goodyear Eagle GTs, unique silver-beige color upholstery and decals with graduated fade-away stripes on the hood blister and lower body sides.

235. As the new Corvette factory commenced operations in Bowling Green, Kentucky, in 1981, the type of paint used was a base coat-clear coat enamel.

Base coat-clear coat was a new paint technology that was supposed to be more durable. Clear coats are generally less vulnerable to chemical attack because they contain no pigment and they absorb UV radiation, which protects the pigmented base coat. The old St. Louis plant would have been too costly to re-equip with this method of painting, which was more environmentally friendly, so it was closed.

236. After previous experience with a limited edition, Chevrolet realized that there are those nefarious types who create "bogus" limited editions to hype the value of their used Corvette. To foil counterfeiters in 1982, Chevrolet put an identifier code into the VIN number of Collector Editions.

Like the Indy Pace Car of 1978, the 1982 Collector Edition was a separate Corvette model, but this time identified as such in the VIN. It's hard to believe anyone can be fooled, but, before the Internet, people didn't have instantaneous access to facts on cars unless they had the right reference book. Now there are websites for many collector editions, and a prospective buyer can check the websites out, including some devoted to various year pace cars. A total of 6,759 Collector Edition 'Vettes were sold by Chevrolet in 1982.

237. Bill Mitchell, the second man ever to hold the post of VP in charge of styling at GM, always liked European headlamps like French-made Marchals, Cibies or British-made Lucas. He had them installed on various Corvette prototypes. In 1979 the first glimmer of advanced lighting finally appeared on the production Corvettes.

Tungsten-Halogen lamps were phased in for the high beams only that year. For many years, American enthusiasts had to live with the fact that Federal law required all headlamps to be 1930s technology sealed beams. That put Americans far behind the Europeans in night lighting.

238. The fastback window on the '78 that replaced the previous "tunnel-back" roof must have been popular because Chevy sold 47,667 Corvettes in 1978. Chevrolet wisely installed a roll-type security shade.

If you remembered to use it, it at least made your luggage less vulnerable to "window-shopping" thieves.

239. The hatchback's first year on the Corvette was 1982.

It was a boon in utility but it was only offered on the Collector Edition, adding a certain measure of exclusivity to the special model.

240. The '82 was the Corvette's first for the lock-up torque converter.
The lock-up feature of the 700R4 4-speed automatic operated on all forward gears except first, making the automatic more efficient. It used a higher first gear ratio (3.07:1) for better acceleration off the line. There was no manual transmission available that year.

The C4 Era

241. Stung by criticism that their HD suspensions weren't as sophisticated as those from other countries, Delco tied in with Bilstein in 1984 to develop a shock absorber especially for the new generation Corvette.
The Delco-Bilstein shock was the high gas-pressure deCarbon type. It was available as a separate option (FG3) in 1984 or as part of the Z51 suspension package. Dick Guldstrand had raced a Camaro in 1982 and 1983 with Bilsteins and demonstrated to Chevrolet their superiority over what they were using.

242. In 1984, one of the features premiered by Chevrolet on the '65 Mako Shark II show car finally made its appearance on a production Corvette. This feature was a clamshell hood that lifted part of the fenders with the hood.
The idea was to show off more of the engine, which it did indeed. But it also greatly added to the expense of crash repair, a situation somewhat remedied in the C5 when they went back to a traditional hood separate from the fenders. The rear window slats never reached production on the Corvette, though, Shinoda, when he went to Ford, used a variation on the Boss 302 Mustang.

243. In 1984 Chevrolet turned to a surprising source for their manual gearbox for the Corvette—a former drag racer gearbox maker named Doug Nash. His gearbox was called "4-plus-3" overdrive.
The name came because it was basically a 4-speed Super T-10 but with an overdrive you could activate on the top three gears, which gave you seven ratios in all. Nash merely bought the Super T-10, tooling and created this "new" gearbox, using an add-on overdrive unit. Parts are now in short supply.

244. The brakes for the '84 came from Girlock Ltd.
It was a bit surprising, Chevrolet choosing an Australian firm, but then Girlock—a joint venture of Girling and Lockheed—had been developing brake systems for many years in Australia.

245. In 1984 option CC3 was a see-through roof. It was made of acrylic plastic.

In hot weather states, i.e. Arizona, they can't see a need for a see-through roof that makes a car like a toaster-oven but in cold weather states like Michigan, a see-through roof makes winter weather more interesting. Bill Mitchell had see-through roofs on several Corvette show cars so blame the production option on his inspiration. The option cost $595, and over 15,000 were sold in 1984.

246. Goodyear Eagle VR50 high-performance tires made their debut on the '84 Corvette.

V-rated for speeds over 130 mph, it was nicknamed "Gatorback" because the curved horizontal grooves suggested scales on an alligator's back. They were designed to be unidirectional with a preferred rolling direction.

247. The drag co-efficient of the '84 was touted highly at introduction. It was 0.34.

This was a pretty good figure, but in ten years, even sedans were occasionally pulling better in the wind tunnel. The '84 was wind tunnel tested but nothing like the next generation to follow.

248. The year 1987 was the Corvette's first for roller valve lifters.

Time was in Corvette history when, if they found roller valve lifters on a Corvette after it won a race, the driver would be disqualified. But now Chevy made them available as standard because they minimized friction losses, which increased fuel mileage by 3% and power by 5 hp.

249. The code number for the stiff suspension, i.e. the "Performance Handling Package" available in 1984 was called the Z51.

The 6-foot, 1-inch author distinctly remembers bouncing his head on the ceiling after hitting a bump in a Z51-equipped '84. So let the buyer beware on those '84s. Fortunately, it was softened a bit in 1985.

250. Chevrolet built 56 Corvettes for the Corvette Challenge.

They sent fifty over to a shop to have roll cages installed. The engines were taken out, and sealed engines installed to equalize the "challenge" between drivers and not engine builders. You could have your original engine reinstalled once you left the series. Six more cars were built but not fitted with the roll cages, maybe for spares.

251. The L98 came along in 1985.

It still displaced 5.7 liters but compression was higher and it had Bosch port fuel injection. It was rated at 230-hp at 4,000 rpm and produced strong low-end torque of 330 pounds-feet. It also delivered better fuel economy.

252. In 1985 there was a new name for fuel injection on the Corvette. It was "Tuned Port Injection" (TPI).
Central intake runners replaced the cross flow manifold of the old "Cross Fire" system that went back to 1982. The relatively long inlet runners created a strong torque peak at 3,200 rpm, but limited top end power. A bonus was the fact that the new name reminded one of a "tuned" induction system for a racing engine.

253. In 1986, the body style that had its premiere in 1984 finally got a ragtop.
ASC, a company started by Heinz Prechter in Detroit, helped engineer the convertible top and, for their effort, was rewarded the contract for the convertible top, plus a separate contract for a lift-off hardtop, but his firm did not install the convertible tops.

254. Back in the last millennium, the Corvette factory rolled out a number of twin-turbo prototypes. However, the closest they got to offering one for the public was to include a code number on the order form so the Corvette you ordered could be shipped off to a private firm in Connecticut who would install twin turbos for you. The name of this Chevrolet factory-approved maestro of speed was Reeves Callaway.
Reeves Callaway became Chevrolet's version of Carroll Shelby, with Callaway making more exciting vehicles than Chevrolet Division could get GM management to approve. One wonders how many of Callaway's ideas were slipped to him from GM or whether it was the other way around?

255. The first few Callaway-built Twin Turbos built in 1987 used the LF5 Chevrolet block.
If that doesn't sound familiar, look in a truck parts book. The first four Callaway Twin Turbos used truck blocks, the ones with the four bolt main caps. Callaway says they didn't like them and changed to splayed bolt caps ASAP. Callaway reports that the blocks worked fine in the real world nevertheless.

256. The 35th Anniversary Edition Corvette, introduced April 1, 1988 at the New York Auto Show, was known by RPO Z01.
It included white lower body, black roof hoop, transparent black acrylic roof panel, commemorative badges above fender gills, embroidery on the white leather seats, dual 6-way power seats,

GM-Delco Bose stereo, and heated door mirrors. It was not available on the convertible.

257. There were 2,050 35th Anniversary editions sold by Chevrolet in 1988.

It was ironic that, back in 1978, Chevrolet angered dealers by originally not planning on making at least one Anniversary car for every dealer but ten years later, it was no longer an issue and the dealer body seemed happy that only just 2,050 Anniversaries were made. Maybe the dealers had realized that, the fewer there are of a limited edition, the more they could charge for the ones they had.

258. 12 Callaway Speedsters were made.

The Paul Deutschman-designed open car, with its wraparound window treatment and aerodynamic body panels inspired by earlier Callaway specials like the Hammer, was originally projected to be part of a limited edition of 50. Only twelve were made—ten Twin Turbo pushrod cars and two ZR1-based Twin Turbo Super Speedsters with 750-hp. When Chevrolet changed from the C4 to the C5, it no longer made sense to build out the Speedsters based on the now out-moded body design and chassis.

259. Chevrolet built factory racing Corvettes for the public? No, we're not talking the Grand Sports of 1963. Starting in 1988, Chevrolet actually built a short run of Corvettes for SCCA with stock matched horsepower engines that were sealed to prevent teams from modifying them. The goal was to have all the engines be of equal power so the series would be a true contest of driving talent alone. The series was called the Corvette Challenge Series.

The series was very successful. It demonstrated the reliability and fun driving that could be found in the nearly stock Corvette. Ferrari later copied the entire concept to market Ferraris. Most of the Corvette racers had their engines changed during the season in the hopes of getting more closely matched engines in horsepower.

260. Sales of the Callaway Twin Turbo were under 70 in 1989.

The real number Callaway reports selling that year was 69 Twin Turbos. The numbers were falling, especially since the public was anticipating the ZR1, a car with 170-mph speed capability that didn't need a turbo. Another figure sometimes cited for 1987 is 184 made.

261. Most Corvette fans will say the King Kong of C4 generation Corvettes was the 4-cam ZR1. Others favor the Callaway Twin Turbo. If you look at the year 1990, when the ZR1 was introduced, the Callaway Twin Turbo put the ZR1 to shame on torque.

It was the Twin Turbo by a bunch—562 ft-lbs at 2,300 rpm compared to the 4-cam LT5's 370-ft-lbs at 4,500 rpm.

262. The Corvettes in the Corvette Challenge Series ran different wheels than the Corvettes sold in the showrooms. The manufacturer was Dymag.

The British-made wheels had been used first on Corvettes by Callaway.

263. In 1989, the Corvette got a 6-speed gearbox, model MN6, as a no-cost option. It was made by the German supplier, ZF.

Nicknamed "Zed-Eff" in proper Deutsch for the name of the company Zahnradfabrik Freidrichshafen, ZF is a famous firm that has made gearboxes for most of the premium sports cars in Europe including Aston Martin.

264. In 1989, the purpose of the 6-speed manual ZF's "bypass" feature was to force you to "short shift" from 1st to 4th in order to reduce emissions to meet "CAFÈ" (Corporate Average Fuel Economy) emissions standards.

The Chevrolet Motor Division, like all other carmakers in the U.S., were under pressure to reduce emissions and improve fuel economy. The best way to do this was to force the driver to use fewer gears. The system was set up so that, if you were dawdling along when you upshifted, i.e. weren't accelerating hard enough, it "blocked out" or forced you to bypass 2nd and 3rd gears, leaving 4th gear as your next option. It's a good thing that the engine has lots of torque.

265. In 1989 Chevrolet built between 80-100 ZR1 Corvettes.

The key word is "production." They built them but not for sale. They were used in evaluation, for photography and by the media (including a trip to Europe to show how they worked on European roads). One explanation is that, if they couldn't supply enough to meet full demand, they might as well postpone availability until the 1990 model. Similar considerations back in 1953 forced restricted delivery that year. Rumors persist that at least one LT5-powered '89 "mule" has been found in a British junkyard and re-imported to its homeland.

266. In 1989, the tri-mode suspension was only available on coupes with a manual gearbox and Z51 handling package. The option code number for the variable choice Selective Ride and Handling Control was FX3.

At $1,695, it was an expensive electronically-controlled system. Even though it required the Z51 package, the springs and anti-roll bars were from the softer '88 Z52 package for a wider range of suspension control. The only exception was the 60 Corvette Challenge cars built in 1989 that had FX3 suspensions coupled with Z51 springs and stabilizer bars.

267. The Lotus-designed 4-cam Corvette engine was built for Chevy by Mercury Marine.

Chevy projected 4,000 units a year, too small an amount for GM to establish in-house facilities. It's not that unusual to go outside for a limited run. Even Chrysler in the glory days of the 426 Hemi assembled those engines at their Marine Division. GM hoped to reap many benefits out of buying Lotus, but this engine was about the only tangible benefit they got after several years of trying to squeeze ideas out of their British "think tank."

268. In 1990 there was another racing series for Corvettes, which Chevrolet again built cars for. In this one you could build the engine yourself or buy it prepared from Chevrolet. It was called the "World Challenge."

The name was changed from the previous "Corvette Challenge." In this series you could buy a racing engine from Chevy or build your own. The cars had heavy-duty springs and the FX3 Selective Ride & Handling system. Reportedly only 23 were built.

269. The concept Corvette that came out of the GM's California design studio, the Advanced Concept Center (ACC), was called the Stingray III.

The show car was seven inches longer in wheelbase than a C4, and three inches wider, but 2 inches shorter overall because it cut out the usual Corvette overhangs. Its styling influenced the Chevrolet Cavalier more than the C5.

270. A feature that the LT5 shared with the L98 was bore centers.

The original hope was that the new design would share some parts with the pushrod engines to save money, but once they got deep into the project, the higher engineering standards of the LT5 made that impossible. The pushrod V-8 was still relatively crudely finished compared to the Swiss watch-like LT5. At least with the same bore centers it could be installed from the bottom at the factory like the L98. Sometimes assembly line convenience is the most important factor.

271. In 1992, the LT1 engine had reverse flow cooling.

Ordinarily water goes to the block first and then to the heads. Chevy "thought outside the box" when they decided to have the coolant pumped first to the heads and then the block. This increased bore temperature for reduced ring friction and improved cooling around the valve seats and spark plug bosses.

272. In 1992, the Goodyear GS-C tires on the Corvette were asymmetrical.

Long before, by shooting pictures through plate glass of tires driving over them, tire engineers had found that tires had more pressure put on them on one side than the other, but it wasn't until the 1990s that they began building tires with a different tread pattern on one side than the other to take advantage of this. They were uni-directional as well.

273. The rear wheels on the ZR1 were 11 inches wide.

The wider wheels, carrying P315/35 ZR17 tires, were the reason it was necessary for the ZR1 to have a wider body section in the rear than its pushrod kin. Besides the wider rear body, Chevrolet also gave the ZR1 exclusive squared taillights, which they then made nonexclusive by making them standard on all Corvettes in 1991.

274. The official nomenclature for the four-cam engine offered in the Corvette was LT5.

Although it was confusing to those not familiar with option codes, for many years in the Corvette, Chevrolet used the prefix "L" to designate an engine, such as L48, and the prefix "Z" to designate special performance equipment packages such as Z06 of 1963 or the ZR1 of 1990.

275. In 1986, in a real departure, Chevrolet agreed to run off a special limited edition of fifty Corvettes to honor a specific dealer. The Commemorative Edition had its own special two-tone paint job. The honored dealership was Malcolm Konner Chevrolet.

Automakers will sometimes deviate from the norm when you place a big enough order, which is why those Mary Kay representatives keep driving those pink Cadillacs. This car was built to commemorate Mr. Konner, who as far back as the 1950s had been a champion of the Corvette.

276. Chevrolet used Lotus to test experimental features on their mid-engined Corvette Indy prototype. The "secret weapon" Lotus fitted their prototype with was Active Suspension, which GM thought would change auto history.

While the "Active Suspension" worked well in Lotus' race car, it didn't work as well in the Corvette GTP race car and GM gradually concluded it was way too complicated for production cars. Infra-red night vision did come to GM but was offered on Cadillac first (and we thought Corvette was the GM car to get the new stuff first!).

277. In 1992, there was a new generation small block introduced, recalling the name of a great engine in the Corvette's past. It was called "LT1."

This was in honor of the great high-revving LT1 of 1970. The new engine produced 300-hp at 5,000 rpm. It had a redline of 5,700 rpm, 700 more than the L98.

278. "Direct-Fire" was the marketing name chosen for the new "distributorless" engine in the Corvette.

By this time, the names "Astro" and "Turbo" no longer had such magic. It worked as described, using four coils, each firing two plugs simultaneously, all controlled by the ECM which computed spark advance based on engine speed, manifold pressure, throttle position, and coolant temperature plus a signal from the crankshaft position.

279. It is a little known fact that several (as many as a dozen) LT5-powered convertibles were built for testing purposes. However, Chevrolet decided the convertible lost too much rigidity to be able to handle the increased power and there was worry the top would be ripped off by the wind blast at 160 mph. Nonetheless, GM official Don Runkle was presented with a custom-styled 4-cam Corvette convertible as a personal gift.

Although he was presented the silver car with yellow leather interior by the Design staff in a public ceremony, Runkle, then head of Advanced Engineering, didn't get to enjoy it for very long. Perhaps in a move designed to discourage future executives from receiving similar gifts, GM took the car away. In contrast with the "privileges of rank" attitude of 1960s era executives like Bill Mitchell, the new company policy was not to let experimental cars get out into private hands.

280. In 1992 the new Traction Control System came from Bosch. Called "Acceleration Slip Regulation," it worked by automatically reducing throttle opening or applying rear brakes to fight wheel slip. It could be shut off by a console button if you insisted on doing a little "burn out."

281. The DOHC LT5, in its first incarnation, produced 125-130-hp more than the pushrod L98. And it was all done without resorting to supercharging, turbocharging or nitrous oxide! The four-cammer was more efficient in terms of breathing with such niceties as four valves per cylinder and a 3-valve throttle body. Power was rated at 375-hp vs. 245 or 250 for the L98. The L98's dual power rating was a result of two different muffler systems, which were determined by transmission and axle choice.

282. Pittsburgh Plate Glass, a huge auto industry supplier, sponsored dozens of pace cars as PPG Pace Cars at CART-races. At least two Corvette pace cars were built. A blue one was based on a C4 chassis and body of a convertible, with the emergency strobes built into the hefty roll bar. A purple one was built on a non-stock chassis, and had a longer nose than a Corvette, and somewhat crude bodywork. This one had a strong resemblance to the obscure Giugiaro-designed Corvette-powered Bizzarrini SRL targa, of which only two were built, but one of which has been resident in Detroit since it was new.

283. The ZR1 had, of course, its own special engine, its wider wheels and tires, and its own unique rear styling for one year. There was also something unusual about the glass—it had a solar windscreen that cut down on heat load entering. With a large expanse of glass and less underhood space for A/C equipment, it was important to reduce the total solar gain and hence, demand on the A/C unit.

284. ZR1s came with a key-operated switch, which, if activated by the owner, cut the power output in the car to 250-hp. This fiendish device was designed to dampen the enthusiasm of valets. It was called the "valet key" and worked by locking out the second stage power boost, but the device didn't stop valets from putting the pedal to the metal if given the opportunity. Some owners report it was more effective on wives, making them think it was a tamer car than it was.

285. In 1993, the PASS key system was replaced by the Passive Keyless Entry (PKE) system.

Michael Antonick, Corvette historian, says the previous system was too confusing to owners. The new one sounded the horn when you locked the car with the fob transmitter.

286. There were 1,344 of the higher horsepower second-generation ZR1s sold once they could brag about having 405-hp.

Not a very big number out of 6,939 ZR1s sold. Unfortunately the boost in horsepower didn't help sales. The economy was recovering from a significant recession, collector car prices were tanking, and demand for the once mighty ZR1 was fading fast.

287. On July 2, 1992, in Bowling Green, Kentucky, a white Corvette roadster with red interior rolled down the assembly line. It marked the 1,000,000th Corvette built.

Chevrolet deliberately arranged for the 1,000,000th car to be white with a red interior to show the continuity of the original concept. The headrests also had unique embroidery proclaiming the car's historical status.

288. The ZR1 had a lot of power when it was introduced. Port and polish was one of Chevy's hot rodders' tricks to get additional horses.

The major change was to use the old hot rodder's trick of hand porting the heads, which netted them an additional 30-hp.

289. In 1992, Dave Hill was named the new Corvette Chief Engineer.

Only the third Corvette Chief Engineer in the marque's first 47 years, Hill came to the Corvette from Cadillac. His predecessors were Duntov and McLellan. His "Corvette achievement" beyond finishing the development of the C5 was the 2001 Z06 fixed roof coupe.

290. The 1993 40th Anniversary (RPO Z25) package-equipped Corvettes are collector's items all by themselves. If you had access to a time machine, you should go back in time and order the ZR1 option with your 40th Anniversary to make sure it's even more of a "keeper."

The four-cam would make it more valuable for sure, but in this case ordering one optional package atop the other would be pricey. Let's see, $34,595 for the base coupe. Add $31,683 more for the ZR1 and throw on a mere $1,455 more for the 40th anniversary package. Only 245 ZR1s were thus honored.

291. On the 1996 Grand Sport RPO Z16 package, the width of the rear wheels on the coupes was 11 inches (the convertible was 10.5 inches).

The coupes enjoyed wider wheels than the convertibles when you ordered the Grand Sport package for a practical reason: if you got a flat with the wide wheels and had been running them on the convertible, you couldn't fit the deflated big tire and wheel in the convertible's storage space. Chevy made the wider tires legal by adding small flares to the coupe's rear wheel wells.

292. Due to painting difficulties, the color Copper Metallic turned out to be extremely rare in the 1994 Corvette.

The paint color-coded 66 on the option list proved quite difficult to apply evenly. Because of this it was dropped early in the game with less than 120 released.

293. On Sept. 2, 1994 the National Corvette Museum opened to the public in Bowling Green, Kentucky.

The Museum often plays host to special shows and continuously displays Corvette prototypes on loan from GM and private owners.

294. In 1996 the LT4 optional engine had several features that made it more desirable than the LT1. However, an automatic transmission was not one of these features.

In a step reminiscent of the old days when the highest performance engines were not available with automatics, the LT4 was not available in 1996 with an automatic. This saved on the number of drivetrain combinations GM had to certify for emissions.

The C5 Era

295. When the C5 was introduced in 1997, it had no spare tire.

The decision to have no spare was controversial but the new run-flat tires by Goodyear made a spare unnecessary since you can travel on a deflated tire for over 200 miles at 55 mph.

296. The first prototype of the Corvette Indy show car had a twin turbo engine made in Europe by Ilmor.

The initial concept showed a 2.6-liter CART-spec. V-8 engine fitted with twin turbos instead of the single seat race car's single turbo. Later they decided the production Corvette would have a 4-cam V-8 designed by Lotus. Chevrolet financed the development of the Ilmor "Indy" engine for CART, and that engine carried the Chevrolet name on the cam covers.

297. The C5 Corvette, which premiered in 1997, had one ingredient that any boy who grew up in the 1950s would recognize. It was the balsa wood core in the floorboards.

Balsa wood was used by kids in the 1950s to make model airplanes. Reportedly, the specially-sourced balsa wood from South America proved superior when tested against synthetic composite materials for a combination of strength and sound attenuation properties. Never mind that it put the Corvette in the same class as Morgan in one respect—as one of the few automakers still using wood as a structural element.

298. In the case of the '98 Indianapolis 500 Pace Car, the car came fairly "loaded" ("optioned out"). Some remaining options that you still had to pay extra for if you wanted them on your Pace Car replica were a front license plate holder, remote compact 12-disc CD changer, body side moldings, magnesium wheels, and a 6-speed manual.

The just over $5,000 price of the Pace Car replica option package (ordered on the base convertible which itself cost some $44,000 plus) didn't represent as big a price premium as the '78 Pace Car package, which added roughly 25% or more to the cost of the car. So in that way, the '98 Pace Car was more of a bargain. But will it be as collectible?

299. In 1998, 1,163 Pace Car replicas were made.

A rather surprising amount considering the insistence by Chevrolet that every Pace Car replica have the "Boy Racer" graphics all over them instead of shipping the decals in a separate package for the owner to apply as they did back in 1978. Some owners have devised a way to remove the decals, most doing this leaving just one small one on each side to prove the car's Pace Car origin. What this will do to the long-range re-sale remains to be seen...

300. New colors in 2000 included Dark Bowling Green Metallic and Millennium Yellow.

Chevrolet felt they just had to acknowledge their first Millennium. The second new color name was obviously a politically correct way to honor the city where the Corvette's newest plant was located.

Bibliography

All the books below were consulted by the editor, or by the proofreaders, or even by correspondents being polled on the internet websites run by Corvette Forum and NCRS. All of the book titles listed below that are currently in print are available from Motorbooks International (Classic Motorbooks) Osceola, Wisconsin, whose number is accessible on the internet.

Adams, Noland, *Complete Corvette Restoration and Technical Guide* , Vol. 1, 1953-through-1962

Adams, Noland, *Complete Corvette Restoration and Technical Guide* , Vol. 2

Adams, Noland, *Corvette American Legend 1954-55 Production (History Series No. 2)*

Adams, Noland, *Corvette: American Legend 1956 Racing Success (History Series No. 3)*

Adams, Noland, *Corvette: American Legend: The Beginning (History Series No. 1)*

Adams, Noland, *Corvette: American Legend (History Series No. 4)*

Adler, Dennis, *Corvettes: the Cars that Created a Legend*

Antonick, Michael, *The Corvette Black Book 1953-2000*

Antonick, Michael, *Illustrated Corvette Buyer's Guide*

Brigermann, Chuck, *Essentials, A Corvette Collector's Guide*

Dobbins, M.F. *Fact Book of the 1968-1992 Stingray*

Ethan, Eric, *Corvettes (Great American Muscle Cars)*

Falconer, Tom, *Essential Corvette Sting Ray: The Cars and Their Story 1963-67*

Falconer, Tom, *Early Chevrolet Corvettes 1953-'67*

Falconer, Tom, *Original Corvette: 1953-62*

Haines, Shirley, *Corvette: The American Sports Car*

Langworth, Richard, *Complete Book of Corvette*

Leffingwell, Randy, *Corvette: America's Sports Car*

Lentinello, Richard A., *Corvette (Autofocus Series)*

Ludvigsen, Karl, *Corvette: the American Legend*

Ludvigsen, Karl, *Corvette: The Exotic Experimental Cars*

Mueller, Mike, *Corvette 1953-'62*

Mueller, Mike, *Corvette 1968-1982*

Mueller, Mike, *Corvette C5*

Mueller, Mike, *Corvette Sting Ray 1963-1967*

Newton, Richard, *How to Restore and Modify your Corvette 1968-1982*

Porter, Lindsay, *Chevrolet Corvette Restoration Guide*

Prince, Richard, *Corvette Restoration Guide 1968-1982*

Wyss, Wallace, *Corvette Prototypes and Showcars Photo Album*

Another Great Book!

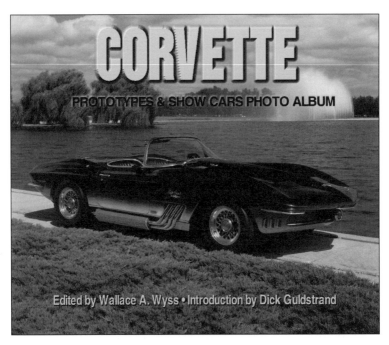

Corvette
Prototypes & Showcars
Photo Album

By Wallace A. Wyss. Introduction by Dick Guldstrand. From the first Corvette to the Sting Ray III. Softbound, 112 pgs, 10 1/4" x 8 1/2", 146 B&W photos, ISBN 1-882256-77-8. Item No. 10070A, $19.95.

All books available through:

Iconografix, Inc.

PO Box 446/BK,
Hudson, Wisconsin, 54016
Telephone: (715) 381-9755,
(USA) (800) 289-3504,
Fax: (715) 381-9756

Another Great Book!

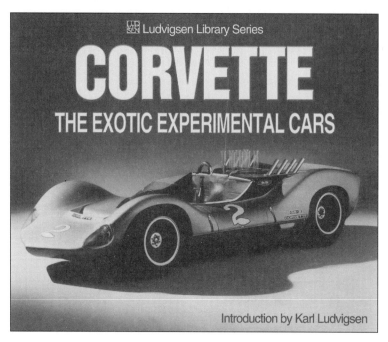

Corvette
The Exotic Experimental Cars
(Ludvigsen Library Series)

Introduction by Karl Ludvigsen. Behind the scenes of Chevrolet R&D and Design Staff. Softbound, 128 pages, 10 1/4" x 8 1/2", 119 B&W photos, ISBN 1-58388-017-8. Item No. 10106A, $19.95.

All books available through:
Iconografix, Inc.
PO Box 446/BK,
Hudson, Wisconsin, 54016
Telephone: (715) 381-9755,
(USA) (800) 289-3504,
Fax: (715) 381-9756